Trends of Change
in the Bhakti
Movement in Bengal

Other Titles in the Series

Social Science across Disciplines is a
new series that brings to a general audience
a selection from the papers and lectures
delivered at the Centre for Studies in
Social Sciences, Calcutta (CSSSC), over
the last four decades. They fall into two
categories—first, a selection from among
the Occasional Papers circulated by the
Centre's faculty, and second, from the two
series of memorial lectures in the name of
Sakharam Ganesh Deuskar (for lectures on
Indian History and Culture) and of Romesh
Chunder Dutt (for lectures on Political
Economy).

Hitesranjan Sanyal

Trends of Change in the Bhakti Movement in Bengal

Introduction by
Gautam Bhadra

Centre for Studies
in Social Sciences, Calcutta

OXFORD
UNIVERSITY PRESS

OXFORD
UNIVERSITY PRESS

Oxford University Press is a department of the University of Oxford.
It furthers the University's objective of excellence in research, scholarship,
and education by publishing worldwide. Oxford is a registered trademark of
Oxford University Press in the UK and in certain other countries.

Published in India by
Oxford University Press
2/11 Ground Floor, Ansari Road, Daryaganj, New Delhi 110 002, India

First Edition published in 2019

ISBN-13 (print edition): 978-0-19-948670-0
ISBN-10 (print edition): 0-19-948670-0

ISBN-13 (eBook): 978-0-19-909562-9
ISBN-10 (eBook): 0-19-909562-0

Typeset in Berling LT Std 10/14
by Transtics Data Technologies, Kolkata 700 091
Printed in India by Replika Press Pvt. Ltd

Contents

About the Author

Hitesranjan Sanyal (1940–1988) studied Ancient Indian History and received his PhD from the University of Calcutta. He was Fellow in History at the Centre for Studies in Social Sciences, Calcutta (CSSSC) from 1973 to his sudden and untimely death. His book *Social Mobility in Bengal* was published in 1987. *Bangla Kirtaner Itihas* (1989), on the history of the Vaishnava musical form of *kirtan*, and *Swarajer Pathe* (1993), his collected essays on the nationalist movement in Bengal, were published posthumously, as was his *Selected Writings* (2004) containing his essays on temple building and architecture.

About the Editors

Partha Chatterjee is Professor of Anthropology and of Middle Eastern, South Asian and African Studies, Columbia University, New York. A member of the CSSSC faculty for thirty-six years, he was also its Director from 1997 to 2007 and continues as Honorary Professor of Political Science. Among his books are *Nationalist Thought and the Colonial World* (1986), *The Nation and Its Fragments: Colonial and Postcolonial Histories* (1993), *A Princely Impostor? The Strange and Universal History of the Kumar of Bhawal* (2001), *The Politics of the Governed* (2004) and *The Black Hole of Empire* (2012).

Rosinka Chaudhuri is Director and Professor of Cultural Studies at the CSSSC. She is also the first Mellon Professor of the Global South at the University of Oxford. She has written *Gentlemen Poets in Colonial Bengal* (2002), *Freedom and Beef Steaks* (2012), and

The Literary Thing (2013) and edited *Derozio, Poet of India* (2008), *The Indian Postcolonial* (co-edited, 2010), *A History of Indian Poetry in English* (2016), and *An Acre of Green Grass and Other English Writings of Buddhadeva Bose* (2018). She has also translated and introduced *Rabindranath Tagore: Letters from a Young Poet* (2014).

About the Introduction Writer

Gautam Bhadra was educated in Presidency College, Calcutta, and Jawaharlal Nehru University, New Delhi. After teaching for several years at the University of Calcutta, he was Professor of History at the CSSSC from where he retired in 2010. He was a founder-member of the Subaltern Studies collective. He is the author of several books in Bengali on peasant revolts, social and cultural history, and the history of publishing in Bengal. He received the Ananda Purashkar in 2011.

General Introduction to the Series

Partha Chatterjee and *Rosinka Chaudhuri*

This series of publications from Oxford University Press brings to a general audience a selection of the papers and lectures delivered at the Centre for Studies in Social Sciences, Calcutta (CSSSC), over the last four decades. They fall into two categories: first, a chosen few from among the Occasional Papers circulated by the Centre's faculty and second, from the two series of memorial lectures in the name of Sakharam Ganesh Deuskar, for lectures on Indian history and culture, and Romesh Chunder Dutt, for lectures on political economy.

The CSSSC was founded in 1973 as an autonomous research institute financed primarily by the Indian Council for Social Science Research and the Government of West Bengal. Since then,

General Introduction to the Series

the Centre, as it is ubiquitously known, has established an academic reputation that places it at the crest of research institutes of excellence in India. Its faculty works in the fields of history, political science, sociology, social anthropology, geography, economics, and cultural studies. Its unique interdisciplinary culture allows for collaborations between scholars from different fields of research that might not find support in traditional department-based institutions, attracting students and researchers from across the country and abroad.

The R.C. Dutt Lectures at the CSSSC have focused on themes from economic theory, economic history, and development policy, mostly relating to India. As is well known, Romesh Chunder Dutt (1848–1909) served in the Indian Civil Service from 1871 to 1897. On retirement, he lectured at the University of London, UK, and wrote his classic work in two volumes, *The Economic History of India under Early British Rule* (1902) and *The Economic History of India in the Victorian Age* (1904). He was elected president of the 1899 session of the Indian National Congress. Apart from his extensive writings on the colonial economy, the condition of the peasantry, famines, and land rights, Dutt was also a poet in English and a novelist in Bengali, writing on historical and social themes. Over the years, some of the most eminent economists of India have delivered the R.C. Dutt lectures at the Centre. Among them are Sukhamoy Chakrabarti, K.N. Raj, V.M. Dandekar, Ashok Rudra, Krishna Bharadwaj, A. Vaidyanathan, Suresh Tendulkar, Prabhat Patnaik, I.S. Gulati, Amit Bhaduri, C.T. Kurien, Praveen Visaria, Kaushik Basu, Geeta Sen, Debraj Ray, Abhijit V. Banerjee, Ravi Kanbur, and Dilip Mookerjee. The lectures selected for publication in the present series will capture key debates among Indian economists in the last four decades in topics such as the crisis of planning, economic liberalization, inequality, gender and development, sustainable growth, and the effects of globalization.

The S.G. Deuskar Lectures began as a series on Indian nationalism but widened to reflect the cross-disciplinary interests the CSSSC nurtured, featuring a range of distinguished speakers on the history, culture, politics, and society of India. Sakharam Ganesh Deuskar (1869–1912) was Maharashtrian by ancestry and member of a family that migrated in the mid-eighteenth century to the Santal Parganas on the border of Bihar and Bengal. A schoolteacher and journalist by profession, he is best known for his Bengali tract *Desher Katha* (1904)—a damning indictment of the exploitative and violent character of British colonial rule—which is reported to have sold 13,000 copies in five editions within five years during the Swadeshi movement in Bengal. Some of the finest scholars and artists of modern India have delivered the Deuskar Lectures, including, among historians, Ranajit Guha, Tapan Raychaudhuri, Irfan Habib, Satish Chandra, Romila Thapar, Partha Sarathi Gupta, Sabyasachi Bhattacharya, Sumit Sarkar, Dipesh Chakrabarty, Muzaffar Alam, Gyanendra Pandey, Sanjay Subrahmanyam, and Shahid Amin; among philosophers, J.N. Mohanty and Bimal Krishna Matilal; among artists and art critics, Geeta Kapur, Vivan Sundaram, K.G. Subramanyan, and Ghulam Mohammed Sheikh; among social theorists, Gayatri Chakravorty Spivak, Sudipta Kaviraj, and Veena Das. A selection of these lectures will now be reprinted in this current initiative from Oxford University Press.

Occasional Papers published by the CSSSC represent the research of the CSSSC faculty over the years. Many of these papers were later published in journals and books, some becoming classic essays that are essential reading for students and researchers in the field. Some of the most important works in the Indian social sciences, it would be fair to say, are represented here in the form of papers or drafts of book chapters. Of the nearly 200 Occasional Papers published so far, we will reprint in the present series only those that are not already in wide circulation as journal articles or book chapters. Included among our Occasional Papers will be the current initiative of the Archives Series Occasional Papers, meant specifically to showcase the collection in the CSSSC visual archives.

By turning these outstanding papers into little books that stand on their own, our series is not intended as a survey of disciplinary fields. Rather, the intention is to present to the reader within a concise format an intellectual encounter with some of the foremost practitioners in the field of humanities and social sciences in India. R.K. Narayan, in his childhood memoir, *My Days* (1947), had written that when, as young men, he and his friends had discussed starting a journal and were thinking of names for it, someone suggested 'Indian Thought'. 'There is no such thing' was the witty response from a friend. Narayan nevertheless began publishing *Indian Thought*, a quarterly of literature, philosophy, and culture, which lasted all of one year. We suggest that this series might, in the end, prove his friend wrong.

Introduction

Gautam Bhadra

The devotional Bhakti movement, or more specifically, the Vaishnava Bhakti movement, in Bengal is a subject on which much has been written since the time of its founder, Chaitanya (b. 1486). Articulate and organized, Vaishnava devotees have themselves produced a rich archive, comprising theological treatises and biographies, as well as dramas and poetical works such as the performative *pada* or verse, written in Sanskrit and in the vernacular languages. A large number of historical and literary works in the nineteenth and twentieth centuries also contain criticisms and reassessments of the Chaitanya movement in Bengal, representing continuing efforts to rework its achievements and limitations, sometimes within the framework of rational inquiry and on other occasions as an emotional quest. Within this long tradition of discussion and debate, some academic scholars, such as Jadunath Sarkar, Dineshchandra Sen, Bimanbihari Majumdar, Bhupendranath Dutta and Sasibhushan Dasgupta, have made notable contributions on various aspects of the movement since its beginning in the period of the Bengal sultans. Each of these scholars had a distinct approach, focusing on specific themes in the making of Gauriya Vaishnavism. Sushil Kumar De's work *Early History of the Vaisnava Faith and Movement in Bengal* (1942) and Ramakanta Chakravarti's *Vaisnavism in Bengal (1486–1900)* (1985) stand out because of their comprehensiveness and historical overview of the movement from its inception to the recent past. Sushil De was interested in drawing fine delineations among various stances within Vaishnava theology, whereas Ramakanta Chakravarti has underlined the historical role of the Vaishnava heritage in forming various social institutions and cultural traditions in Bengal.

In line with these earlier approaches, Hitesranjan Sanyal (1940–1988) tried to spell out his own distinctive opinion regarding Vaishnavism in Bengal. His work remained unfinished because of his untimely death. The present Occasional Paper, partially published in *Bengali Vaisnavism: Orientalism, Society and the*

Arts (1985) edited by J.T.O'Connel, is an early statement of his original thinking and analysis of the transformation of the regional Bhakti movement in Bengal. Being a Gandhian, Sanyal had a particular orientation in his historical quest to identify the characteristics of Bengali culture. He did extensive research on the social history of temple building as well as on rural mobilization during the Gandhian movement in Bengal. His search was always for locating particular sites of creative and collective initiative from below and their interaction with various influences, directions and pressures emanating from centres of authority and peer cultural groups. The present paper fits squarely within the Gandhian temperament of his project.

Sanyal has clearly distinguished between two centres of the Gauriya Vaishnava movement: 'Gauramandala' in the Rarh region of Bengal, i.e., the south-western region, particularly the western side of the Ganges-Bhagirathi river system, focusing on Navadvip, and 'Brajamandala', focusing on Brindaban. Based on a simple *bhakti* towards the persona of Chaitanya as the focus of supreme devotion, without recourse to ceremonies, Nityananda and his followers built a theory of *Gaura-paramyavada*. By contrast, Rupa, Sanatana, and Jiva Gosvami worked out an elaborate theology and hierarchical structure of authority at Brindaban, based on *baidhi* (conforming to the sastra) and *raganuga* (emotive) Bhakti: this resonated with the systemization of an all-India Bhakti movement with its emphasis on the absolute spirit of Krishna as the supreme object of veneration. To them, devotion to Chaitanya is *upeya* or means for achieving the final goal (*upaya*) of a mystic reunion with the supreme God, Krishna. In Sanyal's opinion, one approach does not necessarily negate the other; rather the Gosvami *siddhanta* (doctrine) has been grafted on local Vaishnava initiatives, negotiating, accommodating, and on their terms, changing the spirit in the writings, activities and performances of the devotees. At the same time, Sanyal has pointed out how 'excessive' and unorthodox practices in numerous sects have resisted and coloured the rigour of the Gosvami authority at the top. The twists and turns in the relationship between 'Gauramandala' and 'Brajamandala' have permeated all the articulations and forms of Vaishnavism in medieval Bengal.

In fact, in the long duration of the active life of Bengali Vaishnavism until today, it may be argued that Vaishnavism, as a movement, had multipronged and differential impacts, each impact producing its own effect on the culture of a particular place. Hitesranjan Sanyal has an awareness of this differential impact—an awareness evident from his scattered writings on social mobility and temple building. The highly sanskritized *naisthika* (orthodox) Gosvami school strengthened the local zamindar's power and pomp, resulting in the upward mobility of many intermediate social groups and the spread of a literary culture among the peasant community. In the middle, the intersection of orthodox and heterodox Vaishnava beliefs and theology evolved into an ideology of daily social practices well-suited for the *grihastha* or householders, who could negotiate among one another and interact with the roaming preachers or *vairagi*. In the seventeenth century, these interactions produced the institution of the *akhra* (hospices) and the *mela* (gatherings for seasonal Vaishnava festivals). The unorthodox practices, with their insistence on the adoration of Radha and the doctrine of *parakiya* (intense longing for other's wives as an ideal) and the amorous *lila* (play) of Krishna, gave birth to many small esoteric spiritual sects and local ideological formulations where androgynous themes played a distinctive role. The twists and turns in the ideologies and aspirations of various social groups and *pashanda* (heretic/unorthodox) sects have permeated all articulations and forms of Vaishnavism in medieval and modern Bengal.

One should note that the present paper is a small part of Sanyal's broader study of various types of musical performances or *kirtana* in the Bengali Bhakti movement. The first fruit of his extended research is available in *Bangla Kirtaner Itihas*, posthumously published in 1989. Inspired by the works of Nirmal Kumar Bose and Niharranjan Ray, he has always tried to place the specifics of region and locality within the broad contour of a bigger cultural site. Yet it is evident that his sympathy lies for local initiatives. He has not denied the efficacy and necessity of directions and influences from above, but his yearning is for the *desi* (indigenous) and homemade colours in the heritage. In his opinion, local initiatives form the basis of regional cultural self-confidence, an absolute necessity to fight every form of parochialism. Vaishnava culture, for him, stands for an emotional make-up that goes beyond the networks of patronage and power and creates a space for an individual within the *mandali* or collective. The history of this formation of the emotional world of medieval Bengal still remains largely unwritten. Sanyal's small brochure would be a right beginning for that venture.

Trends of Change in the Bhakti Movement in Bengal

HITESRANJAN SANYAL

I. Introduction

Bengal experienced a great efflorescence of culture between the fourteenth and the seventeenth centuries. There occurred at this time phenomenal development of the Bengali language, literature and script and of distinctive styles of architecture, sculpture and painting. In course of this cultural growth, culture traits of Bengal developed into what may be called a regional Bengali identity. The process of cultural growth was largely inspired by the Bhakti movement led by Sri Krishna-chaitanya popularly known as Chaitanyadeva (1486–1533) and its successor, the Gauriya Vaishnava *sampradaya*, i.e., sect. Some trends of change could be noticed, however, within the Bengali regional traditions of *bhakti* from the fifteenth to the seventeenth centuries. Such trends transformed the original character of the Bhakti movement and ultimately shaped the social character of the crystallized Gauriya Vaishnavism.

Initially, Vaishnavism was revitalized in Bengal by Sri Chaitanyadeva whose spiritual fervour places him among the greatest protagonists of the Bhakti movement, such as, Vallabhacharya, Ramananda, Kabir, Nanak and Sankaradeva. However, one can demarcate at least two phases in Chaitanya's spiritual career. In the first phase he was a householder in Nabadwip and exerted considerable influence on the different strata of people in his native town. In this phase of his preaching, Chaitanya gave a broad democratic flavour to the Vaishnava outlook by organizing unceremonial but intensely emotional devotional congregations in a spirit of fraternity. This is one of the principal reasons for the tremendous appeal of *bhakti* in Bengal. *Sannyasa* marks the second phase of Chaitanya's life when he lived in Puri in Orissa. During this phase Chaitanya emphasized the discipline of soul through devotion, in Radha-like spirit, to his beloved aspect of God, Krishna, and developed an inclination for canonical interpretation of the faith propounded by him. Chaitanya does not appear to have taken any positive step to organize a sect. But what was significant was his attempt to share out responsibilities among his associates. He instructed his principal associates of the Nabadwip base, particularly Nityananda, to concentrate on mass preaching of simple, unceremonial *bhakti* in Bengal. On the other hand, Chaitanya deputed two associates from the court elite of Bengal, the Karnat Brahmans, Sanatana and Rupa, to develop the canonical literature of *bhakti* in the heartland of Vaishnavism, at Brindaban near Mathura. Sanatana and Rupa were the foremost among the celebrated six Gosvamis of Brindaban. It was the extensive intellectual and spiritual efforts of the Gosvamis by which Gauriya Vaishnavism was systematized.

The growth of the endeavours of the Gosvamis in what is known among the Vaishnavas of Bengal as Brajamandala, as distinct from Gauramandala, the territorial core of Bengal Vaishnavism, brought the latter in touch with the broader subcontinental forces of Indian spiritual tradition, both of the Ganga plains and Karnataka. The Bhakti movement was now more affected by the hierarchical tendencies and social and cultural authoritarianism which are implicit in the medieval Indian religious tradition. Jiva Gosvami, the youngest among the six Gosvamis of Brindaban, deputed three Bengali disciples to go back and disseminate the new principles of Brajamandala in Bengal. One of these disciples, Narottamadasa, settled in the village of Kheturi (in Rajshahi district) on the Bangladesh bank of the Padma opposite Lalgola and undertook extensive journeys through the region in order to communicate with the leading *Mahantas* of the Bhakti movement. Then he instituted a *mahotsava* at Kheturi to which came representatives of the various groups of Vaishnavism who had been inspired by Chaitanya. Out of this assembly crystallized the form of social and ideological community, *sampradaya*, which enunciated the seventeenth century principles of Gauriya Vaishnavism.

Sampradaya identity in the Bengali regional form of the Bhakti movement was the social product of the changes described earlier. Its pristine democratic flavour gave way to relatively narrower and more hierarchical practices, which gave it a sectarian character. Such trends, with their own regionally specific circumstances of origin and development, may be found in the kind of sectarian solidarity which developed in varying degrees in the

Sankaradeva orders in Assam or among the Kabirpanthis, the Satnamis or the Sikhs. These forces of change leading to sectarian developments within the Indian religious tradition also indicate the process of social and cultural change in the different regions of India. In the following pages, an attempt will be made to focus on these forces and the changes which they brought about in developing the Bhakti movement of Bengal into the Gauriya Vaishnava *sampradaya*.

II. Characteristics of the Regional Bengali Culture

The process of the emergence of Bengali regional idioms in the sphere of organized and systematized cultural activities had begun in the eighth century during the regime of the Pala monarchs (eighth century to twelfth century). This is indicated by the Eastern Indian school of scultpure and painting and the developments in the fields of language, literature and script since the eighth century. But these developments represented regional versions of the pan-Indian culture (as it was visualized in the Indian traditions since the second century B.C.) which despite being in a process of decline since the eighth century continued to be the most influential factor in the cultural life of India. The territory through which those developments took place was much larger than the present Bengali-speaking region. Between the eighth century and the twelfth century, Bengal formed but a part of the larger Indian cultural region which covered the area between south Bihar and Assam and included the north–eastern part of Orissa as well.[1]

By the middle of the fourteenth century, the Bengali-speaking territory had come to be roughly demarcated from the neighbouring cultural regions. In this region, the influence of the pan-Indian normative culture persisted. Besides, with the advent of the Muslims at the beginning of the thirteenth century, West Asian culture traits began to spread in Bengal. In spite of these influences, indigenous Bengali elements had tended to come into prominence in the sphere of organized cultural activities in Bengal. From the fourteenth, and through the sixteenth, century the indigenous elements emerged as the dominant factor in the cultural life of Bengal, and determined the terms of interaction between indigenous traits and external influences. This is indicated by the modifications of the *Ramayana* and the *Srimad-bhagavat* in terms of the regional ideas and idioms in the Bengali translation and adaptations of these texts on the one hand and the literary transformation of folk tales on the other.[2]

A more convincing evidence of this trend is provided by the regional Bengali architectural style as represented by the *chala* type of temple which developed since the middle of the fifteenth century. The basic lines of the architectural design of the low, curvilinear *chala* hut which is associated with the peasant culture of Bengal was adopted for designing the exterior of the *chala* temple. The fragile *chala* form was rendered into a permanent structure with the help of the advanced technique of arcuation which was introduced in India by the Muslims. But despite the tremendous potentialities of the technique, arcuated constructive principles had been made completely subservient to the unpretentions and simple form of the *chala* design.

There are indeed many limitations of the regional style of *chala* architecture characterized by the distinctive features of the hut architecture. The limitations are both structural and aesthetic. But the regional style of architecture had two important features. First it was the inherent capacity of the indigenous culture to absorb and assimilate, in the process of its growth, elements from high cultural traditions. The second notable feature is the confidence generated by the growth of the regional cultural traits: the symbols and idioms of the regional Bengali culture were indigenous in origin and character.[3]

III. Bhakti Movement of Bengal: Regional Self-confidence Expressed in Simple, Direct *Bhakti*

In the context of the growing regional Bengali identity, the Bhakti movement launched by Chaitanyadeva exerted tremendous influence on the Bengalis since the early decades of the sixteenth century. Chaitanya preached simple and direct faith or *bhakti* (devotion). Deep and inseparable absorption in Krishna will lead to *prema* (love) for him. Every individual irrespective of caste, sex, lineage and learning has the inherent capacity for acquiring such unqualified, wholehearted *bhakti* to Krishna. The means of arousing the inward emotion of total absorption in Krishna is the simple, unconventional and non-ritualistic *nama-samkirtana*, i.e., reciting the name of God. *Nama-samkirtana* can be done both severally and collectively in a spirit of fraternity and fellowship.[4]

The sense of freedom and fellowship propagated by the Bhakti movement is but a manifestation of the urge for self-assertion generated by the growth of the regional culture. The focus on the unconventional, non-ritualistic way of simple worship, congregational *nama-samkirtana* in the Bhakti movement and its emphasis on the inherent capacity of the individual irrespective of caste, sex and social standing catered to the socio-cultural needs of the common people. Chaitanya and his close associates appear to have been aware of this fact. At the early stage of his religious career in Nabadwip, Chaitanya moved round the quarters of the artisans and traders in the town and mixed with them.[5] At Advaita Acharya's behest, Chaitanya promised to devote himself to the task of spreading the message of *bhakti* among women, Sudras and the illiterate.[6] This was also the avowed objective of Nityananda, who was the most influential and energetic preacher of the Bhakti movement and the main reason for the tremendous success he had achieved in his mission of preaching.[7]

The emphasis on the lower rungs of society had another important dimension. At the time when Chaitanya launched the Bhakti movement there existed in Bengal several esoteric sects.[8] They included the adherents of Tantric practices, Buddhist, Sakta or Saiva, the Kapalikas, Abadhutas, and the Natha *yogis*. The Tantra-based sects, commonly referred to as Sahajiyas, and the cognate sects like the Kapalikas, had grown around the contemplation of the relationship between the male and the female principles in the nature of the Ultimate Reality. Their method consisted in secretive sexo-yogic practices adopted as the means to attain transcendental bliss leading to supreme knowledge. The esoteric sects were widely prevalent in Bengal and commanded large followings. But at the level of the organized upper strata of society regulated by the norms of the canonical *marga* or *sastriya* tradition, the sexo-yogic practices of the esoteric sects were hardly recognized as respectable forms of religious exercise. One reason for this was the extreme esotericism of the sexo-yogic practices. Another reason may be found in the attitude of these sects towards Puranic Brahmanism and Mahayana Buddhism.

The esoteric sects straightaway rejected the authority of the established religions and scorned their ceremonial rites and rituals as well as the recondite learning of the canonical texts, i.e., the *sastras*.

The Bhakti movement led by Chaitanya offered the followers of the secret esoteric sects an opportunity to come out in the open and join the fraternity of the Krishna devotees without compromising the fundamental tenets of their religious faith. The basic doctrine of the esoteric sects centres around the concept of duality as expressed by the male and the female principles in the nature of the Absolute; perfect union of the two is the highest truth, the Absolute Reality. The ontological principles of male and female are inherent in the physical state of man and woman. Therefore, in order to know the Absolute Truth, man and woman should unite together physically, mentally and spiritually and realize their true nature in a state of transcendental bliss. As such, the esoteric sects rejected conventionalism and ceremonialism and scrupulously abhorred high thinking and deep learning. Truth, they affirmed, is a matter of intuition.

The apparent division of the Absolute Reality into *saktimat* (possessor of power) and sakti (manifestation of power) as symbolized by the duality of Krishna and Radha and the relation of love between the two constitute the central theme of Chaitanya's religious idea. Chaitanya sought to realize the nature of the spontaneous love between Krishna and Radha and the nature of their union at the emotional level through mystic experience. Such an approach may not have been entirely conducive to the religious practices of the esoteric sects but the doctrinal compatibility tended to validate their ideology in a broad-based religious movement in which the different strata of society participated. Besides the direct and simple faith of Chaitanya, its strong emotional appeal and the unconventional, non-ritualistic method of worship which promoted a sense of freedom and fellowship attracted the adherents of the esoteric sects to the Bhakti movement. Thus the Krishna Bhakti movement offered the followers of the esotoric sects an opportunity to assert themselves openly. A large number of Sahajiyas had joined the Bhakti movement and had acquired an eminent position in it. Narahari Sarkar of Srikhanda[9] and Bansibadana Chatta[10] were prominent Sahajiya associates of Chaitanya. Svarupa Damodara was one of the closest associates of Chaitanya. The Sahajiya Vaishnavas trace the lineage of their *gurus* from Svarupa.[11] Raya Ramananda, who was a very close associate of Chaitanya in Puri, has been characterized as a Sahaja Vaishnava in the *Chaitanya-chandrodaya* by Kavi Karnapura.[12] The participation of the Sahajiyas in the Bhakti movement expanded its social base.

Bengal appears to have come under the religious and cultural influence of north India since the time of the Mauryas (fourth century to second century B.C.). Vedic religion, Puranic Brahmanism, Buddhism and Jainism had come to Bengal through its north India connections. There had developed in Bengal a few important centres of the different religions. But, till the sixteenth century, Bengal had looked towards north India for sources and models of religion and culture. Some of the Siddhacharyas exerted considerable influence on the followers of the secret religious cults and had composed songs and poems to explicate the ideas of their sects. But the influence and achievements of the Siddhacharyas did not have any impact on the organized level of religion and culture.

Between the thirteenth and the sixteenth centuries almost the whole of India was swept by a surge of the Bhakti movement. The origin of the concept of *bhakti* may be traced back to the Upanisads. Subsequently, it developed into a versatile cult marked by a kind of liberal heterodoxy which was distinguished by a sense of freedom and fellowship. Especially related to Vaishnavism, the *bhakti* cult emerged as a viable alternative to the orthodox aspect of Puranic Brahmanism and absorbed the tradition of esoteric meditation which prevailed outside the sphere of organized religion. It constituted a powerful parallel trend in the religious life of Hindu society almost all over India. Thus the concept and the cult of *bhakti* constituted a common pan-Indian heritage. But the Bhakti movement that developed in different parts of India, for instance in Maharashtra, Karnataka, Bengal, Assam, Bhojpur and Punjab, emphasized different aspects of the cult and was permeated with strong regional characteristics. In Bengal, the movement was launched in Nabadwip under the leadership of Chaitanyadeva. The movement was inspired by *Krishnabhakti*, i.e., devotion to Krishna, who was considered to be the sole object of worship. The devotees cherished unqualified and wholehearted devotion of *premabhakti* to Krishna. Chaitanya himself longed for union with Krishna. But to the devotees of Bengal, Chaitanya was not only the embodiment of intense devotion to Krishna but was Krishna himself. Thus Chaitanya was the supreme object of worship. Even before Chaitanya renounced the worldly life to become a sannyasi (ascetic) in 1510, the devotees of Nabadwip had come to be convinced of his oneness with Vishnu and Krishna. In Nabadwip, Chaitanya was worshipped by his prominent associates as being Vishnu himself, the Supreme Being.[13] This was followed up by the devotees of Chaitanya with the introduction of *Chaitanya-kirtana*, the hymn for chanting the name of Chaitanya.[14] Apparently, the name of Chaitanya was considered to have the same spiritual potential as the names of Hari (Vishnu) and Krishna, which were chanted in *nama-samkirtana* as the means to attain *premabhakti*.

The concept of Chaitanya's selfhood as Vishnu has been crystallized and elaborated in the writings of Murari Gupta, Prabodhananda Sarasvati, Svarupa Damodara, Kavi Karnapura and Brindabanadasa, all of which are datable between the second and the third quarters of the sixteenth century. Murari refers to Chaitanya as *bhagavan svayam*, i.e., God himself.[15] Prabodhananda explicitly says that the worship of Chaitanya is more desirable than the worship of Krishna.[16] Karnapura indicates that God appears in the person of Chaitanya.[17] Brindabanadasa identifies Chaitanya with Krishna and focuses on the divinity of the Master from the time of his birth.[18]

Svarupa Damodara, a close associate of Chaitanya, is known to have composed a theological text called *Gauratattva-nirupana* in which he propounded the *panchatattva* doctrine. The doctrine regards Chaitanya and his four principal associates of the Nabadwip circle, namely, Nityananda, Advaita Acharya, Sribasa and Gadadhara Pandita, as the manifestations of the five different aspects of the Supreme Reality but focuses on Chaitanya as the Mahaprabhu, the Divine Self, and hence the greatest of all.[19] In his *Gaura-ganoddesa-dipika*, Kavi Karnapura has described a complete hagiology of the faith and has elaborated the *panchatattva* doctrine.[20] The contemporary poets who composed *padas* (Bengali lyrics) also regarded Chaitanya as Krishna himself as well as both Krishna and Radha in one personality.[21]

The concept of Chaitanya (fondly called Gaura or Gauranga for his bright and fair complexion, particularly with reference to his Nabadwip career) being the *Parama-tattva*, i.e., the Supreme Reality, inevitably led to the theological position of *Gaura-paramyavada* which signifies the adoration of Chaitanya as the supreme object of worship.[22] As the logical concomitant of *Gaura-paramyavada* there developed the iconography of Chaitanya as also *Gaura-mantra*. Even during the life time of Chaitanya his image was consecrated and worshipped by his devotees in Bengal. The practice spread after the demise of the Master.[23] Some of the *Gaura-paramyavadis* replaced the *Gopalamantra* (the formula for invoking the grace of Gopala, i.e., Krishna) by *Gaura-mantra* in spiritual initiation of disciples and in ritualistic worship.[24]

The Sahajiyas had devoloped their own versions of *Gaura-paramyavada*. These are known as *Rasaraja sadhana* and *Gaura-nagarabhava*. According to the Sahajiyas, the Absolute Reality, i.e., *Sahaja* is the *Rasa*, the supreme emotion of love, the quintessence in everybody. *Sahaja* articulates itself in its two aspects, namely, *Rasa* (the enjoyer) and *Rati* (the enjoyed) who are conceived by the Sahajiya Vaishnava as Krishna and Radha. The union between the two produces the state of supreme love in *Sahaja*. As the Absolute Reality, Krishna is the Rasaraja. Chaitanya being Krishna himself is also worshipped as Rasaraja. The Rasaraja doctrine was propagated by Bansibadana Chatta of Kulia who may have inherited it from his father Chhakari.[25] But the doctrine has been explicated in a text called *Bansi-siksha* by Premadasa which was composed long after the time of Bansibadana. In this text Bansibadana has been referred to as 'the enjoyed' in relation to Chaitanya.[26]

According to the doctrine of *Gaura-nagarabhava* and the complimentary doctrine of *Nadiya-nagari*, the devotee considers Gaura as the *nagara* (enjoyer, lover) and himself as the *nagari* (enjoyed), a young woman overwhelmed by spontaneous and deep attraction for Chaitanya and running after him in intense desire for love. The young women of Nabadwip are described as having fallen in love with Chaitanya in the same way as the Gopis of Brindaban did in relation to Krishna. Thus Nabadwip is as holy as Brindaban where Krishna performed his lila (divine exploits).[27] *Gaura-nagarabhava* is indicated in the *Sri Chaitanya-chandramrita* by Prabodhananda Sarasvati.[28] It was elaborated in the *padas* composed by Basu Ghosh, Madava Ghosh and Narahari Sarkar of Srikhanda, the founder of the *nagarabhava* group of devotees and in the *Chaitanya-mangala*, a biography of the Master composed by Narahari's disciple Lochana.[29]

The emergence and spread of *Gaura-paramyadava* indicate that the Bhakti movement led by Chaitanya had enhanced the self-confidence generated by the growth of the regional Bengali culture, and that Chaitanya had become the symbol of Bengali self-confidence. It is important to note that Chaitanya and the ideology of the Bhakti movement appealed to both the upper and the lower strata of the society. On the one hand, Chaitanya's associates included scholars, poets, musicians and other highly placed persons belonging to the upper castes. On the other hand, the message of the Bhakti movement exerted tremendous influence on the lower rungs of society even at the early stage of Chaitanya's religious career in Nabadwip. As Nityananda and the other associates of Chaitanya had brought into the movement the people from the lower social strata including the Doms and the Chandalas who constituted the lowest rungs of the caste hierarchy.

IV. Emergence of Brindaban as the Alternative Focus of the Bhakti Movement of Bengal: Systematisation of Faith and Ideological Modifications

Chaitanya does not appear to have taken any positive step to build up a system or a sect. But there are indications to suggest that he seriously pondered over the future of the Bhakti movement and adopted certain measures to ensure its growth. Several centres of the Bhakti movement had grown in Bengal. In those centres, preaching was led by Nityananda, Advaita, Gadadharadasa, Narahari Sarkar, Bansibadana and Sivananda Sena who were among the original circle of devotees around Chaitanya in Nabadwip which formed the nucleus of the Bhakti movement. Although Chaitanya had left Bengal after becoming an ascetic and had settled down in Puri in Orissa, he exerted broad control on his associates and followers preaching in Bengal. It was at his behest that Nityananda carried out extensive preaching among the common people along the banks of the Ganga.[30] On the other hand, Chaitanya took the initiative in organising in Brindaban a centre for intensive intellectual and spiritual exercise related to the Bhakti movement.

It is with this intention that Chaitanya diverted some of his brilliant associates to Brindaban. He specifically instructed the two illustrious brothers, Sanatana and Rupa, to settle down in Brindaban in order to revive the sacred places associated with the *lila* (divine exploits) of Krishna and to compose *bhakti-sastra*, i.e., canonical texts on various aspects of *bhakti*.[31] Later they were joined by Gopala Bhatta, Raghunatha Bhatta, Raghunathadasa and Jiva, who was a nephew of Sanatana and Rupa. Collectively these six recluses are known as the *sharagosvami*, the six Gosvamis or teachers of Gauriya Vaishnavism.[32] Sanatana, Rupa and Jiva, who were men of great intellectual and literary capacity, had devoted themselves to the lifelong mission of scholarly and spiritual pursuits. Sanatana wrote on *rasa-sastra* (canons of devotional sentiments) and Rupa composed texts on theology. Jiva, who was a prolific and versatile author, reinforced the ideas of his uncles by his penetrating metaphysical works. To these works was added a voluminous compilation by Gopala Bhatta, probably in collaboration with Sanatana, in which the social and religious practices of the Vaishnavas had been codified. Together, the four Gosvamis systematized the faith and defined the canons of what later came to be known as the Gauriya Vaishnava *sampradaya*. Due to this reason, the four Gosvamis have been held in highest veneration as the most authoritative teachers of the Gauriya Vaishnava *sampradaya*.[33]

The faith of the relatively liberal, heterodox Bhakti movement had a very strong appeal for the masses. But the Bhakti movement in Bengal suffered from certain disadvantages and drawbacks. There existed considerable divergences among the prominent associates of Chaitanya even during the lifetime of the Master. Nityananda was the most dynamic among the *Bhakti* preachers and hence had a large following. But there were many detractors of Nityananda. For example, Advaita Acharya strongly disapproved of Nityananda's unconventional personal behaviour and methods of mass preaching.[34] There were others in the Bhakti movement who criticized Nityananda and even refused to tolerate a reference to him.[35] The followers of Advaita constituted a group. They were opposed to both Nityananda and Gadadhara Pandita.[36] The ideas and attitudes of the *Gaura-nagaravadis* were intensely disliked by the other constituents of the Bhakti movement including the followers of Nityananda.[37] It was the common devotion of all to Chaitanya which held the diverse groups together. After the demise of the Master, the different groups drifted away from each other to establish distinctive identities. Thus, there emerged distinct groups led by Nityananda, Advaita, Narahari Sarkar, Gadadharadasa, Hridayachaitanya and Bansibadana. The relation between the groups was marked by indifference and even animosity.[38]

However, these groups shared certain common features. Basically, they were *Gauraparamyavadi*. For preaching they relied on the emotional appeal of simple and direct faith in *bhakti* to Chaitanya and on concrete hagiographical stories of Chaitanya's life. As a matter of fact, the entire Bhakti movement of Bengal centred around the personality of Chaitanya. The life of the Master and the examples of passionate devotion set by him constituted the most important source of inspiration. Thus, the adoration and worship of Chaitanya was the most important factor of the movement. But the movement remained unorganized and even naive. Much was written in Bengal both in Sanskrit and Bengali on the life and exploits of Chaitanya.[39] But with the remarkable exception of Kavi Karnapura,[40] there was no significant attempt to systematize the ideology of *bhakti* in metaphysical implications or by defining the nature of the devotional sentiments following from the doctrine.

The associates and followers of Chaitanya in Bengal failed to develop a system which could be the alternative source of inspiration and guidance after his death. This may be one of the reasons why the Bhakti movement split up into several groups soon after Chaitanya's death in 1533.

The astute and profound scholarship of the Gosvamis, their co-ordinated efforts and the voluminous canonical works covering the different aspects of *Bhakti-sastra* which the Gosvamis produced presented a sharp contrast to the condition of the Bhakti movement in Bengal.

Apparently, there was a sharp break between the Gauramandala and the Brajamandala. One reason for the break is, no doubt, the absence of a common focus, of a leader who could exert influence with both the preachers in Bengal and the Gosvamis of Brindaban. Another reason may be found in the attitude of the Gosvamis as revealed by the doctrinal position adopted by them. In this regard, the Gosvamis drastically differed from the Bengal preachers, who were predominantly *Gaura-paramyavadi*.

Before getting into this question, it is necessary to say a few words about the background of the Gosvamis and the environment in which they worked. The Gauriya Vaishnava creed was systematized mainly by Sanatana, Rupa, Jiva and Gopala Bhatta. All of them came from orthodox Karnataka Brahman families. The family of Sanatana and Rupa had migrated to Bengal a few generations earlier. But the family retained its exclusive Kannadiga character as distinct from the indigenous Bengali Brahmans.[41] Sanatana, Rupa and their two brothers held high positions in the administration of the Bengal Sultans. Presumably, they led the exclusive life of the nobility.

Both Sanatana and Rupa had come in contact with Chaitanya after he had become an ascetic and left Bengal. Unlike the associates of Chaitanya belonging to the Nabadwip circle, Sanatana and Rupa did not have the experience of the early phase of the Bhakti movement, when the devotees of the Nabadwip circle discerned in Chaitanya the presence of the Supreme Being. At the Nabadwip stage of his career, Chaitanya was, no doubt, inspired by Radha's intense and tormenting love for Krishna and sought to identify himself with Radha as the means for attaining Krishna.[42] But Chaitanya also declared his selfhood as Vishnu and Krishna.[43] Chaitanya's associates of the Nabadwip circle appreciated his *Radhabhava* (attitude of Radha) but were convinced of his identity with the Supreme Being.[44] This was the essential feature of their doctrine and they proceeded to preach *bhakti* with the conviction that God had appeared in the form of Chaitanya in order to propagate *bhakti*. Sanatana and Rupa were not acquainted with the process which promoted tremendous self-confidence in the Bhakti movement. Nor did they participate in the emotionally charged mass preaching of *bhakti*, with its focus on women, Sudra and illiterate people, which was initiated by Chaitanya and his early associates in Nabadwip.[45]

This is also true of Jiva, the nephew of Sanatana and Rupa, Gopala Bhatta and Raghunatha Bhatta. After completing his education in Bengal, Jiva decided to devote himself to religious pursuits and went to Brindaban in order to join his uncles.[46] Gopala Bhatta's family lived in Karnataka.[47] Raghunatha Bhatta was a non-Bengali Brahman and a resident of Kasi.[48] They never came to Bengal and had no acquaintance with *bhakti* preaching in Bengal. Raghunathadasa's father was a high placed official in Saptagram in Bengal. Among the Gosvamis, he was the only Bengali and non-Brahman and had close acquaintance with the Bhakti movement of Bengal.[49]

Jiva and Gopala Bhatta may have just seen Chaitanya at a very early age. Sanatana, Rupa, Raghunathadasa and Raghunatha Bhatta had come in close contact with the Master. But all of them had come to know Chaitanya after he had become an ascetic. With the assumption of the role of a *sannyasi*, Chaitanya's religious attitude appeared to have undergone a very significant change. He no more emphasized his selfhood as Vishnu or Krishna. During the *sannyasa* phase of his life, Chaitanya intensely desired union with Krishna as Radha longed for her beloved Krishna.[50] Theoretically, Krishna and Radha are one and the same, Radha being the transfiguration of the *hladini sakti* (the energy of bliss), one of the three essential powers in the nature of God. The power of bliss is manifest in the form of eternal love because God has in his self two aspects, the enjoyer and the enjoyed. Without the reality of the enjoyed he cannot even realize his own nature as the enjoyer. Hence, Krishna expresses Radha out of his own existence for his self-realisation. The divine Radha has natural, spontaneous and all-pervasive desire for uniting with Krishna, for her entire being essentially flows from the very nature of Krishna. Radha's love is the epitome of devotion to the Lord. As such, Chaitanya sought to integrate with his heart the intense and necessary love of Radha for Krishna. Some of the associates of Chaitanya have seen in him the dual incarnation of the enjoyer and the enjoyed: as Krishna in his inner self and Radha in his overt attitude and behaviour.[51] But it was the *Radha-bhava-dyuti*, Radha's lustre of emotion, which was characteristic of the religious fervour of Chaitanya in the Puri stage of his career.[52] The Gosvamis were acquainted with this state of Chaitanya's mind: his total and unqualified devotion to Krishna. They missed the assertive dynamism of the Master's earlier stage of life which inspired the devotees of the Nabadwip circle and made him the centre of their thought and emotion.

The Gosvamis lived in Brindaban, which is situated in the Ganga-Yamuna doab in Uttar Pradesh. The Ganga valley has been a stronghold of Brahmanical orthodoxy from ancient times. The growth of the heterodox

Bhakti movement between the fourteenth century and the sixteenth century had eroded the influence of Puranic Brahmanism to a certain extent. But by the middle of the sixteenth century, the impact of the liberal *bhakti* ideology had begun to subside. The Bhakti movement in different parts of India had come to be reorganized into distinct *sampradayas* or sects which began to compromise their position with the dominant influence of Puranic Brahmanism.[53] The major all-India Vaishnava sects, such as the Sri, Maddhva and Nimbarka, had their headquarters in the Ganga-Yamuna doab. Some of the later Vaishnava sects, the Vallabhachari and the Ramanandi, for instance, who had grown out of the Bhakti movement, had established the main centres of their activities in the Ganga valley in north India. Before the Gosvamis came to Brindaban, Kasi, Prayag, Mathura and Jatipura near Brindaban contained the main centres of several thriving Vaishnava sects. These sects, most of which had developed considerable organisations with sectarian bias, had spread across different cultural regions of India. On the other hand, these sects were closely related to the political and social establishments from which they received the patronage of the imperial state, the Rajput principalities and the rich landlords and merchants. In Brindaban, the Gosvamis were required to carry on the task of building up an alternative system in such a context. The ideas and attitudes of the Gosvamis were likely to be influenced by these circumstances as well.

Thus, the associates and followers of Chaitanya in Bengal and the Gosvamis of Brindaban worked under different conditions. Such differences could account for the variations in approach and attitude between Gauramandala and Brajamandala. Clear evidence of the difference may be found in the Gosvamis' attitude to Chaitanya. The Gosvamis were, no doubt, inspired by Chaitanya but they rejected *Gaura-paramyavada* which was the central theme of the faith of the associates and followers of the Master in Bengal. According to the Gosvamis, Krishna is the Absolute Reality, the source of supreme love; hence, he is the *upeya* and the main object of worship. The theological and metaphysical systems of the Gosvamis have been built up around the central theme of the love between Krishna and the Gopis. The Gosvamis adored Chaitanya as a great *guru* and the ideal devotee and even implicitly recognized him as the *bhagavana*, i.e., God, but they have never projected him as the *Parama-tattva*, i.e., the Supreme Reality. The Gosvamis looked upon Chaitanya as an *upaya*, i.e., the means of attaining the desired goal, which is access into the land of eternal love wherein resides the Ultimate Reality, rather than an *upeya*, i.e., the Ultimate Reality. Hence, according to the Gosvamis, the worship of Chaitanya is not a valid proposition.[54]

The Bhakti movement of Bengal was launched with the ideal of attaining *prema* (love) which follows from total absorption in simple and pure *bhakti*. Such a state of devotion could be achieved through intense personal experience (*anubhava*) gained by means of *samkirtana*, reciting and chanting aloud the name, form and attributes of God, particularly his blessed name. Brindabanadasa, Lochanadasa and the poets of the *padas* indicate that Chaitanya and his followers considered *kirtana* to be the most important mode of worship which gives rise to *prema*.[55] Kavi Karnapura says that *samkirtana* is the sole means of *bhakti*.[56] According to Jayananda, *kirtana* is the greatest means of spiritual fulfilment.[57] However, according to the Gosvamis, *samkirtana* is a practice of piety in the *vaidhi* (in accordance with *vidhi*, i.e., the injunctions of the *sastra*) variety of *sadhana-bhakti* (devotion attained by means of special extraneous effort). *Samkirtana* is important because it is the most powerful means of effecting a devotional sentiment at the *vaidhi* stage. But its potentials are limited because at no stage does *vaidhi sadhana-bhakti* involve emotional realisation of the devotee's relation with the desired object, *ishta*.[58] This is possible in the other variety of *sadhana-bhakti*, namely, *raganuga*, which is modelled after (*anuga*) *raga*, i.e., the natural, deep and inseparable absorption in Krishna as manifest in the attachment of the people of Braja who stand in actual relation to Krishna as parents, friend, lover or servant. Their attachment represents different *rasas* (devotional sentiments) in accordance with the nature of their relationship with Krishna, such as, *vatsalya* as parents, *sakhya* as friends, *madhura* as lovers and *dasya* as servants. In the *raganuga* way, the devotee adopts one or the other *rasa* as an emotional exercise towards spiritual fulfilment. In fact, as Sushil Kumar De explains:

> The Raganuga Bhakti ... consists of an emotional sublimation of intimate human sentiments towards Krishna, in terms of intimate devotional sentiments displayed by different personal relationships ... between

the deity and his dear ones (*parikara*) in the eternal sport at Vraja. It is thus an ecstasy of vicarious enjoyment in the sense that the devotee does not seek to establish a direct personal contact of his own with the deity, but prepares himself for it by imitating and realizing within himself the different aspects of the beatific sports in terms of one or other of the blissful devotional sentiments; and through years of constant practice he ultimately identifies himself with such sentiments.[59]

Raganuga bhakti was widely prevalent among the devotees of the Nabadwip circle but their approach was different. The difference followed from the concept of Chaitanya's identity with Krishna. With the presence of Krishna among them, the devotees stood in actual relation with the Ultimate Reality. In recollection of Krishna's *lila* (divine sport) in Braja, Nityananda was considered to be Balarama (*sakhya*),[60] Gadadhara Pandita (occasionally Gadadharadasa as well) was considered to be Radha[61] (*madhura*), the *Gaura-nagaravadis* looked upon themselves as *nagari*, i.e., the Gopis, the milk-maids of Braja who were the beloved of Krishna (*madhura*)[62] and several devotees, such as, Gauridasa, Ramai,

Krishnadasa and Paramesvaradasa, adopted the attitude of the *Gopalas* (cow-herd boys) who accompanied Krishna (*sakhya* and *dasya*).[63] They adopted the *bhava* (attitude) of the *parikaras* of Krishna for defining their personal relations with the deity in terms of natural, deep and inseparable absorption in him. Chaitanya's *lila* in Nabadwip is in fact nothing but the same *lila* which Krishna performed in Brindaban.

The idea of direct personal relationship with the Ultimate Reality persisted in Gauramandala even after Chaitanya's departure to Puri. Gradually, the idea was elaborated. The associates of Chaitanya and even their disciples came to be considered as the incarnations of the *ganas* (dear associates) of Krishna. A complete scheme of the reincarnation of the *ganas* of Krishna in the *Nabadwip lila* has been systematized in the elaborate hagiological text *Gaura-ganoddesa-dipika* composed by Kavi Karnapura in 1575.[64]

Vaidhi-bhakti is an important component of the Gosvami system. They emphasized *vaidhi-bhakti* for the benefit of those who remain at the primary stage of religious life. The large compendium called *Haribhakti-vilasa* lays down the rules of formal religious practices in the rites and rituals of *vaidhi-bhakti* and of virtuous conduct of the Vaishnava householder. In dealing with these subjects, the *Haribhakti-vilasa* accepts the efficacy of the caste system and recognizes the superiority and prerogatives of the Brahman in religious and social matters.[65] The text deprecates the Sudra, forbids acceptance of gifts from a Sudra and even suggests that one should expiate if he comes across the sight of a Chandala.[66] The *Haribhakti-vilasa* considers that *diksha*, i.e., spiritual initiation, is absolutely necessary for beginning a spiritual career. The text lays down certain rules in this regard. A Brahman *guru* is always desirable and should be sought after by people belonging to all *varnas*. A Brahman *guru* is entitled to impart *diksha* to lower *varnas*. The *Haribhakti-vilasa* permits a Sudra to act as a *guru*. But it strictly enjoins that under no circumstance can a man of a higher *varna* be initiated by a *guru* belonging to a lower *varna*. However, a Sudra *guru* can only initiate men of his own caste.[67] Thus the *Haribhakti-vilasa* negates the sense of freedom and faternity propagated by the Bhakti movement as upheld by Chaitanya and his associates in Bengal.

Apparently, the Gosvamis had moved away from the ideology and methods which were developed in the early stage of the Bhakti movement in Bengal and continued in preaching the faith in Gauramandala. The Gosvamis did not assimilate into the system built up by them the symbols and idioms of self-confidence and self-assertion generated by the growth of the regional Bengali culture. It is believed that the system built up by the Gosvamis was based on the teachings which Chaitanya imparted to Sanatana and Rupa. *Chaitanya-charitamrita* by Krishnadasa Kaviraja is the only source where one has an account of Chaitanya's teachings to these illustrious brothers.[68] Krishnadasa lived in Brindaban and was closely acquainted with the Gosvamis.[69] He received first-hand information on this subject from the Gosvamis themselves. But Krishnadasa's account appears to be heavily influenced by his intimate knowledge of the texts composed by the Gosvamis.[70] It is, therefore, difficult to ascertain the exact context of Chaitanya's own teachings. But there are certain indications by which a broad idea can be formed in this regard. *Radha-bhava* was the dominant attitude of Chaitanya in the Puri stage of his life, when the Gosvamis came in touch with him.[71] Basically, *Radha-bhava* is devotion in the *raganuga* way. As a matter of fact, Chaitanya's devotional attitude had been permeated with *raganuga* in relation to *madhura-rasa* (devotion as the erotic sentiment), the divine love play between Krishna and the Gopis (particularly Radha), from his Nabadwip days. In view of the aforementioned facts, it may not be unreasonable to suggest that the worship of Krishna as the *Parama-tattva* (Ultimate Reality) was the central focus of Chaitanya's teachings to Sanatana and Rupa and that he had instructed them to concentrate on *raganuga-bhakti* modelled after the attachment of the Gopis who stand in *madhura* relation to Krishna.

The teachings of Chaitanya might have induced the Gosvamis to focus on Krishna worship and to emphasize the devotional sentiment of the Gopis as the model and the source of the *raganuga* way. But the Gosvamis' situation in Brindaban as well may have influenced the ideas and methods propounded by them. The Bhakti movement of Bengal and the influence of Chaitanya were essentially a regional phenomena. The symbols and idioms of the regional Bhakti movement could have no appeal in the other cultural regions of India. In the context of the religious and cultural environment of north India and the broader dimensions within which the existing Vaishnava sects rooted in the Ganga valley operated, the Gosvamis might have found it necessary to outgrow the characteristics of the regional Bengali culture. This may have induced the Gosvamis to endow the system of theology, metaphysics and devotional sentiments contemplated by them with a wider appeal so that the system might cut across the boundaries of regional cultural identity. It is only in this way that the Gosvamis could present their system as a viable alternative to the existing systems of the *Bhakti* cult. A broad-based system could be built up only with Krishna as the central focus or the supreme deity of the faith. Chaitanya could not fulfil that requirement.

The theological implications of Krishna as the Ultimate Reality were established long before the Gosvamis began their work. The *ganas* or *parikaras* of Krishna are the embodiments of his *svarupa sakti* (the power which he possesses by virtue of his ultimate nature). As *jiva*, human beings are the manifestations of his *tatastha sakti* (the power through which all beings are created, accidental power). The *sadhaka* (meditator) being a *jiva* cannot aspire to attain the position of *parikaras* of Krishna. Apparently, the Gosvamis had accepted this established theological position. As such, the *raganuga bhakti* as interpreted by the Gosvamis has a much lesser spiritual significance from the point of view of the common devotees than the manner in which it was understood by the preachers of Gauramandala. The devotees of the Nabadwip circle had taken Chaitanya's identity with Krishna as established by personal experience (*anubhava*). They were inspired by a tremendous self-confidence owing to their intimate relation with Krishna appearing in the form of Chaitanya. From the standpoint of the Nabadwip devotees, *raganuga* consisted of the reenactment of the roles which they had played earlier in the *Brindaban-lila*.

V. Interaction between the Tradition of Bhakti Movement in Bengal and the Gosvami System: Emergence of Syncretic Faith

After the death of Sanatana and Rupa which occurred between 1556 and 1558,[72] Jiva Gosvami came to be recognized as the greatest authority of the Gosvami system. Sometime between 1566 and the early years of the 1570s, Jiva entrusted three promising Bengali students, namely, Srinivasa Acharya,

Narottamadasa and Syamananda Pala, with the mission of propagating the Gosvami system in Bengal.[73] Srinivasa, Narottama and Syamananda had come to Brindaban to study the Vaishnava *sastras* and receive spiritual training under the guidance of the stalwarts of Brindaban. During their sojourn in Brindaban, all of them had become thoroughly conversant with the Gosvamis' creed and developed close intellectual and spiritual acquaintance with the leading personalities of Brindaban, including Jiva.[74]

Srinivasa, Narottama and Syamananda brought to Bengal the creed systematized by the Gosvamis of Brindaban. But the tenets, doctrines and dogmas and the method of worship of the new system apparently varied strongly with the trends that characterized the tradition of the Bhakti movement in Bengal. As indicated earlier, the Bhakti movement in Bengal had split into various groups after the demise of Chaitanya in 1533. But the followers of the Bhakti movement strongly adhered to *Gaura-paramyavada*. The tradition of unconventional congregational worship and the ideas of freedom, fellowship and fraternity were firmly entrenched in them. It is in this context that Srinivasa, Narottamadasa and

Syamananda Pala arrived in Bengal with the task of propagating the creed developed in Brindaban.

Among the three missionaries sent by Jiva, Syamananda Pala concentrated on the border areas between Bengal, Bihar and Orissa.[75] Srinivasa preached in Mallabhum in southwest Bengal and in a few other places and taught *bhakti-sastra*. He also visited a few centres of the Bhakti movement and met the leading Vaishnavas for the purpose of interaction and mutual understanding.[76] But the actual task of reorganizing the Vaishnava movement between the Gosvami system and the tradition of the Bhakti movement was taken up by Narottamadasa.

Narottama settled down in the village of Kheturi (Rajshahi district, Bangladesh). Then he set himself the task of combining the different Vaishnava groups into a co-ordinated course of action. Narottama toured extensively in Bengal and went to Puri in order to visit the important centres of the Bhakti movement and meet the leaders of the different groups.[77] After the tour, Narottama organized a *mahotsava* (literally great festival) for celebrating the installation of six sets of images at Kheturi. It is not clearly known when the festival occurred. But it appears to have taken place sometime between 1576 and 1582.[78] On Narottama's invitation, most of the leading Vaishnavas (*Mahantas*) representing various shades of opinion, including the adherents of the Gosvami system and the Sahajiyas, attended the festival along with their disciples. The *Mahantas* included Jahnava Devi, Nityananda's widow and the leader of his followers; Achyutananda, son of Advaita; Raghunandan, the leader of the *Gaura-nagaravadi* group; Sri Chaitanyadasa who represented the *Rasaraja* group; Hridaya-chaitanya of Kalna, Jadunandana, disciple of Gadadharadasa; and the adherents of the Gosvami system represented by Srinivasa Acharya, Syamananda, Rasikamurari, and Ramachandra Kaviraja.[79] Thus, Vaishnavas belonging to different groups assembled on the occasion of the Kheturi *mahotsava*. It marked the earliest occasion for organizing the adherents of the Gosvami system and the different groups of the *Gaura-paramyavadis* including the highly esoteric Sahajiyas. This effort was made under the aegis of the systematized and canonical system propounded in the voluminous texts composed by the Gosvamis of Brindaban and reinforced by the spiritual authority of the Vaishnava luminaries of Brindaban.

In the presence of this vast congregation of various groups of Vaishnavas and with the approval of the assembled *Mahantas*, Narottama installed six sets of images, five of which represented the divine couple, Krishna and Radha, in their different aspects. The sixth was Gauranga-Vishnupriya representing Chaitanya and his wife.[80] All the images were consecrated according to the rules laid down by the Gosvami texts.[81]

The installation of the Gauranga-Vishnupriya image along with the images of Radha–Krishna according to the rituals prescribed by the Gosvamis, indicate a most interesting aspect of the attitude and efforts of Narottama. The devotees belonging to the Nabadwip circle who formed the core of the Bhakti movement in Gauramandala came under the influence of Chaitanya at the pre-*sannyasa* stage of his life and were devoted to the handsome young man that he was. Apparently, it is due to this reason that the early Bengali *padas* on Chaitanya composed by the poets of the Gauramandala refer to his beautiful young appearance and to the names of Gauranga, Gora or Gaurakisora which are associated with it.[82] The images of Chaitanya which were conceived by the Gauramandala devotees represent Gaura dressed as a respectable and charming young man. The Gosvamis, who had seen Chaitanya in his *sannyasa* life only, invariably refer to his *kativesa* (ascetic's appearance) while adoring the Master in their texts. Naturally, the Gosvami texts do not recognize the existence of Vishnupriya. By installing the Gauranga-Vishnupriya image in Kheturi, Narottama demonstrated the acceptance by the adherents of the Gosvami system of *Gaura-paramyavada*, in other words, Chaitanya's selfhood as Krishna who is the *Parama-tattva* according to the view of the Gosvamis. The appearance of Vishnupriya by the side of Chaitanya reinforced the identification. Vishnupriya is conceived as the consort of Chaitanya in the same way as Radha is the *hladini-sakti* (energy of bliss) of Krishna. The pairing of Vishnupriya with Chaitanya may have been a concession to the Sahajiyas as well. The Sahajiyas had already begun to focus on the *sakti*, i.e., the Female Principle, in Chaitanya.

Two types of *kirtana* songs are prevalent among the Vaishnavas of Bengal. These are *nama-samkirtana* and *lila* or *rasa-kirtana*.

Vaishnava *kirtana* might have originated in the earlier tradition of the Buddhist Sahajiya and Nathapanthi *charya* songs as well as in the *panchali* or *vijaya* songs narrating the exploits of different gods and goddesses.[83] A preliminary form of kirtana might have been prevalent in Bengal before the advent of Chaitanya. But Chaitanya appears to have evolved a distinctive and perhaps an improved form of *nama-samkirtana*, i.e., reciting and chanting the name of God, and gave it a special significance as the principal means of worship with tremendous spiritual potentialities.[84] *Lila-kirtana* is a long narrative song dealing with the exploits (*lila*) of God. A narrative is composed of lyrics written by the Vaishnava poets on a particular episode arranged sequentially and woven into a systematic course of development explicating certain ideas. Narottama is credited with organizing the structure of *lila-kirtana* in accordance with the definition and interpretation of the different *rasas* (devotional sentiments) given by the Gosvamis. Indeed *lila-kirtana* became the most powerful medium of spreading the ideas of the Gosvamis among the common people.

In the Kheturi *mahotsava*, Narottama introduced the *lila-kirtana* designed by him.

Rupa Gosvami has classified *kirtana* into three types, namely, *nama-kirtana*, *guna-kirtana* and *lila-kirtana*, all of which are songs on Krishna or about him.[85] But in the Kheturi festival, Narottama began the proceedings with the preface or *Gaura-candrika*, i.e., songs in adoration of Gaurachandra.[86] The *Gaura-candrika* songs consisted of *padas* pertaining to *Gaura-paramyavada* composed by the poets of Gauramandala. The practice of prefacing *Krishna-lila* by *Gaura-chandrika* represents the idea of identifying Chaitanya with Krishna but with a particular emphasis on Krishna worship. Narottama appears to have projected the same idea by installing a Gauranga-Vishnupriya image along with five Radha–Krishna images. Apparently, Narottama sought to reconcile the Gosvami system with the tradition prevalent in Bengal. He accepted Chaitanya as being equal to Krishna, but with an indication that Krishna is more equal and hence is the main object of worship. This is inevitable because Narottama did not intend to deviate from the Gosvamis whose theological and metaphysical speculations and devotional sentiments had been built up entirely on the basic doctrine of Krishna being the *Parama-tattva*.

The festival of Kheturi offered the Vaishnavas of Bengal the opportunity to know closely the Gosvami system with modifications as envisaged by its adjustments to the tradition of the Bhakti movement of Bengal, with particular reference to *Gaura-paramyavada*. The modified system provided the Vaishnavas of Bengal with what they hitherto lacked, namely, a systematic formulation of their faith in the body of concrete *sastriya* discourse. The Kheturi congregation might have been conceived as a common platform for the different groups of the Bhakti movement to meet each other for interaction and mutual understanding under the influence of the Gosvami system.

Apart from *Gaura-paramyavada*, Narottama adapted to the Gosvami system certain other major features of the Bhakti movement of Bengal which expanded the popular base of his mission. As indicated earlier, Chaitanya had emphasized the immense potential of *samkirtana* as the means of acquiring *prema* (devotion ripened into love for God), the highest state of spiritual experience. But the Gosvamis considered it to be merely a religious practice with limited significance. Notwithstanding the views of the Gosvamis, Narottama affirmed the immense spiritual potentialities of *nama-kirtana*. According to Narottama, one can transcend all worldly limitations by means of *nama-kirtana*. Following Chaitanya, Narottama firmly declared that even the lowliest is entitled to perform *nama-kirtana* in his own right. It can be performed at any time and at any place without any spiritual guidance.[87] This may be construed as a negation of the injunctions of the *Haribhakti-vilasa* which prescribes *vaidhi-bhakti* for the common laity and considered spiritual initiation by a *guru* as indispensable.

The *Haribhakti-vilasa* has upheld the validity of caste hierarchy in religious matters. But in pursuance of the tradition of the Bhakti movement in Bengal, Narottama disregarded caste restrictions in his preaching mission. In the Kheturi festival, the Chandalas, one of the lowliest castes of Bengal, were received with great consideration.[88] Narottama was a Kayastha, a Sudra caste of Bengal. In spite of the specific injunction of the *Haribhakti-vilasa* prohibiting a lower-caste *guru* from imparting initiation to an upper-caste person, Narottama initiated several Brahman disciples.[89] Syamananda, who was born in a lower Sudra caste, also initiated higher-caste devotees including Brahmans.[90] Considerable commotion was generated by Narottama initiating Brahmans. In the context of the tension, a conference was held at Kheturi in which many Brahman scholars were present. In this conference, which endorsed Narottama's right to initiate Brahmans, Srinivasa and Birachandra, the sons of Nityananda, who succeeded Jahnava as the head of the followers of Nityananda, announced that a person who had attained devotion to Krishna was greater than a Brahman.[91] This position closely resembles the views of Chaitanya.[92]

Another important aspect of the efforts of Narottama and his colleagues is their enthusiastic promotion of *manjari sadhana*, a highly esoteric mode of meditation. *Manjari sadhana* follows from the elaboration of the *raganuga* meditation as conceived by the Gosvamis. Krishna unites with Radha, who is the transfiguration of his own *hladini sakti* (energy of bliss) as a natural process. In their *lila* (divine sport), the divine couple is assisted and protected by a group of young girls, the *sakhis*. They originate in Krishna being the embodiment of his *svarupa sakti* (the power he possesses by virtue of his ultimate nature). Due to this reason, the *sakhis* have in them the motive force of *raga* (spontaneous, deep and inseparable absorption in Krishna) and are *nitya-siddha* (emancipated by virtue of their existence). Thus, the *sakhis* stand in intimate relation to Krishna. According to the complete scheme of the Gauriya Vaishnava hagiology, Radha and Krishna are attended by another group of young maids called *manjari*. Like the *sakhis*, the *manjaris* are manifestations of Krishna's *svarupa sakti*. As such, the *manjaris'* devotion to Krishna is *ragatmika* (essentially flowing from *raga*) and they are *nitya-siddha*. But the *manjaris* rank below the *sakhis* and are subservient to them. In this capacity, the *manjaris* serve Radha and Krishna in their *lila* and enjoy the right to remain with Krishna. But they are not Krishna's *parama-presta* (most dear ones) to which position the *sakhis* belong.

Raganuga bhakti has two aspects, namely, *bahya* (overt) and *antara* (internal). The *antara* aspect, which involves emotional sublimation of human sentiments, is considered to be more efficacious. In practising *antara raganuga bhakti*, the meditator adopts in his mind a *sakhi* or a *manjari* as the ideal of his *siddha deha* (emancipated being) and endeavours to imitate her characteristics in respect of appearance, attitude and function by means of mental exercise so that he can prepare himself for serving Krishna. However, it is better to take resort to a *manjari* rather than a *sakhi*. *Jiva* (phenomenal being) is the manifestation of the *tatastha sakti* (accidental power) of Krishna and hence is actually incapable of adopting the *bhava* (attitude) of those who are dear to Krishna. In view of the limitations of *jiva*, the position of *manjari* is more conducive to his *sadhana*. The meditator may even seek to serve the *manjari*.[93]

All these ideas follow from the Gosvamis' interpretation of *raganuga bhakti* according to which man cannot attain *ragatmika bhakti* but can prepare himself for access to the land of eternal love by following the devotional sentiments of the *parikaras* of Krishna. However, in their canonical texts, the Gosvamis do not refer to *manjari sadhana* as a mode of *raganuga* meditation. Yet there are reasons to believe that *manjari sadhana* originated with the Gosvamis, particularly Rupa and Raghunathadasa. In their devotional compositions, namely, *stavamala* by Rupa and *stavavali* by Raghunathadasa, they have indicated passionate desire to serve Krishna and Radha in various ways. The services they intend to perform include menial services for the divine couple even during their union. These do not fit with the position of the *sakhi* whose duty is to advise Radha and Krishna on the means by which they could meet each other and to protect them from troubles and hazards. As the later sources indicate, menial services are performed by the *manjaris* only.[94] The Gosvamis may also have practised *manjari sadhana*. In fact, Kavi Karnapura and Narottamadasa explicitly state that the Gosvamis had acquired success in *manjari sadhana*.[95]

The concept of *manjari sadhana* was developed into a complete system of meditation by Narottamadasa, Srinivasa Acharya and their close associates and disciples such as Ramachandra Kaviraja. They defined the hierarchy between *sakhis* and *manjaris* with respect to their position *vis-à-vis* Radha and Krishna and distinguished between the types of services that *sakhis* and *manjaris* were supposed to perform. The *manjaris* serve Radha and Krishna in different ways. Their functions include preparing the bed for the divine couple, massaging their feet and fanning them when they are engaged in love-making and to make arrangements for their comfort after union. The *sakhis'* functions are also related to the love of Krishna and Radha. But as indicated by their position of *parama-presta*, the *sakhis* do not remain on the spot when Krishna and Radha enjoy themselves. The inferior position to which the *manjaris* are entitled require them to attend upon the divine couple even during their union.[96]

The *manjaris* hold the position of menials in the service of Radha and Krishna. But spiritually, the position of the *manjaris* has deep significance. They remain in close relationship with the union of the two aspects of the nature of the Absolute Reality, namely, the enjoyer (the male *par excellence*) and his female principle, the enjoyed, and observe the source of the supreme love which the union creates, but never desires to be enjoyed. Through intense emotional identification with the attitude of the *manjari*, the meditator tries to transcend *purushabhimana*, the pride of a male, or more broadly, human instincts. Thus, *manjari sadhana* is a systematic exercise for transforming a highly erotic symbolism into an acute spiritual process towards an understanding of the nature of the Absolute Reality.

Soon after it was introduced in Bengal, *manjari sadhana* became widely prevalent among different sections of Vaishnavas in

Bengal. Numerous *padas* datable to the seventeenth century testify to its popularity. It offered a complete system of meditation in the *raganuga* way related to *madhura rasa* which seems to have been the dominant devotional sentiment in Bengal. *Manjari sadhana* was also compatible with the *raganuga* way of the *dasya rasa* (devotional sentiment of servitude). Indeed, *manjari sadhana* combined with *madhura* a strong sense of *dasya*. But the more important thing about *manjari sadhana* is that it proved to be instrumental in integrating the Sahajiyas to the main trend of Bengal's Vaishnava movement which was organized by Narottama and his colleagues.

Apparently, the ideology of the Sahajiyas was totally incompatible with the ideology of *manjari sadhana*. According to the *raganuga* doctrine, as interpreted by the Gosvamis, phenomenal beings cannot ever attain the position of the divine associates of Krishna; their *sadhana* consists in following the devotion of Krishna's associates. By contrast, Sahajiyas conceive every man and woman to be intrinsically divine in nature because they represent the male and the female principles of the Absolute Reality. By means of sexo-yogic *sadhana*, every man and woman can discern their pure nature as divine self. The union of the divine male and female generates supreme bliss, which is the highest state of spiritual experience because it is in this state that one can realize the ultimate nature of the Absolute Reality. As Shashibhusan Dasgupta has pointed out, the Sahajiyas had undergone a process of change both ideologically and methodologically under the influence of Vaishnavism. The transformation was possible because the Buddhist Sahajiyas had modified the original Mahayana doctrine of Ultimate Reality into a positive state of vacuity and perfect enlightenment which is Sahaja.[97] The Vaishnava concept of the Ultimate Reality is also a "positive state, though of a supra-mental nature of eternal flow of divine love".[98] The Vaishnavas conceived the Ultimate Reality as supreme love which is manifest in the relation between its two aspects, namely, the enjoyer (Krishna) and the enjoyed (Radha). Drawing upon the Vaishnava ideas, the Sahajiyas interpreted the final positive state arising out of the union of the male and female principles, called *rasa* and *rati* in Sahajiya parlance, as the state of supreme love. Transformation of ideology led to a change of methodology. There was, in the Sahajiya Buddhist cult, a tendency towards psychological development rather than emphasis on psycho-physiological yogic practices which constitute a major characteristic of the esoteric sects. The Buddhist Sahajiyas practised yogic control of sex emotions in order to raise the mind to a state at which it can transcend all temporal relations and attain supreme bliss in absolute *sahaja*. Under the influence of Vaishnavism, the Sahajiyas concentrated more on psychological development towards a transcendental spiritual experience.[99]

Manjari sadhana offered the Sahajiyas further opportunities for realizing supreme love through psychological exercise. Pure love arises only when man and woman can realize their true divine self by removing the worldly principles of nescience and grossness through continual and stringent mental discipline. Originally, the Sahajiyas believed that physical union of man and woman is a potential means of attaining *sahaja*. But the aim of the Vaishnava Sahajiyas, at least theoretically, is to eliminate, even at the initial stage, both from the body and the mind, all animal instincts so as to be fit for practising true love. In the Sahajiya Vaishnava writings, "[t]his strictness has ... been frequently emphasised by the condition that a man must completely do away with his nature as a man and transform his nature to that of a woman before he takes the vow of love".[100] In this respect, the Sahajiyas conform to the Gosvami concept that *jiva* (phenomenal being) being the manifestation of the *tatastha sakti* (accidental power) of Krishna, is, after all, *prakriti* (female) and Krishna is the only male and hence the sole object of love. It is precisely at this point that the Sahajiyas come closest to *manjari sadhana*, despite their doctrinal divergences with the Gosvami system. This is suggested because *manjari sadhana* is also a systematic exercise through intense mental discipline to stimulate in man the attitude of *prakriti* and to shake off *purushabhimana* (the pride of being male) as an essential condition for identifying himself with the devotional sentiments of the *manjaris*.

The Sahajiyas, at least a large section of them, had accepted the ideology of *manjari sadhana*. The Sahajiya Vaishnava mode of worship has been systematized by Mukundadasa in the *Siddhanta-chandrodaya*. Mukunda was the disciple of Krishnadasa Kaviraja, the author of *Sri Sri Chaitanya-charitamrita*,[101] who according to Narottama and the Radha–Krishna yogapitha diagram, had achieved success in *manjari sadhana*.[102] Several Vaishnava *padas* (lyrics) pertaining to Sahajiya doctrine have been quoted in the *Siddhanta-chandrodaya* by way of illustration and explanation. Some of these *padas* indicate the transformation of the Sahajiya mode of meditation in terms of *manjari sadhana*.[103] A clearer evidence of the adoption of *manjari sadhana* by Sahajiyas may be found in some of the *padas* by Chhota Vidyapati contained in the Sahajiya Vaishnava text called *Rasasara*. Chhota Vidyapati unambiguously says that the meditator should try to place himself in the environment of Brindaban and follow the Gopis; an attempt to realize *sahaja* in his own person will inevitably take him to the worst of hells.[104] In another *pada*, the poet says that Krishna is the only male, he contains in him the essence of man. The worldly male should conceive himself as *prakriti* (female) and seek the grace of Krishna.[105]

Baghnapara was an important centre of Sahajiya *rasaraja sadhana* led by the descendants of Bansibadana. But the Gosvamis of Baghnapara practised *manjari sadhana* by adopting *Anangamanjari* as the *siddha deha*. Even the later Sahajiya sects, such as the Sahebdhani, which emerged in the eighteenth century outside the sphere of the Gauriya Vaishnava system, adopted the *raganuga* way and the symbolism of *manjari sadhana* as a means to transcend animal instincts.[106]

VI. Epilogue

Narottama and his colleagues reconciled the Gosvami system with the tradition of the Bhakti movement in Bengal, particularly *Gaura-paramyavada*, which was one of the most important symbols of regional Bengali culture and identity. The reconciliation was the crucial factor in the third and final phase of the Bhakti movement in Bengal. It provided different groups within the Bhakti movement with a theoretical and canonical base of the ideology of *bhakti*. On the other hand, it linked them with the mainstream of Puranic Brahmanism and Vaishnavism and their pan-Indian dimensions. Besides, the syncretic approach of Narottama and his colleagues offered the Sahajiyas the opportunity to integrate themselves with the main trend of the Bhakti movement. The Sahajiya sects, as noted earlier, had a very large following among the common people, particularly in the lower strata of society. Integration of the

Sahajiyas consolidated the broad social base of the Bhakti movement. The syncretic approach of Narottama and his colleagues essentially based on the Gosvami system provided the Vaishnavas in Bengal with a standard version of the faith and practices which was acceptable to all. The Vaishnavas belonging to different groups did not merge to constitute a central organisation in the form of a church or a central authority as in the case of the Sri, the Ramanandi or the Vallabhachari *sampradaya*, for instance. But the common acceptance by the different Vaishnava groups of the modified version of the Gosvami system created a sense of community among the Vaishnavas of Bengal who came to be known as Gauriya *sampradaya* after the name by which the followers of Chaitanya were distinguished from the other Vaishnava sects in the context of the Ganga valley and Orissa. *Nishtha* (firm faith and deep attachment) to the canons and rituals of the faith as propounded by the Gosvami system gave rise to the *naishthika* category which represented the standard form of Vaishnavism in Bengal. Within this flourished the *rasika* (seekers of Krishna as *rasa*) Vaishnavas, mostly Sahajiya. They retained some of their original esoteric practices but at the same time functioned as the channel through which the influence of Gauriya Vaishnavism spread to such esoteric sects as the Baul, the Kartabhaja and the Sahebdhani.

The syncretic approach of the final phase of the Bhakti movement sought to rehabilitate Chaitanya as the supreme deity of the faith. But the effort was confined mostly to juxtapose both Krishna and Chaitanya as the *Parama-tattva* without trying to explain the Chaitanya phenomenon in terms of a canonical system. In the absence of a canonical interpretation of the *Gaura-paramyavada*, the doctrine remained as an adjunct to the central focus on Krishna. There was no attempt to systematize Chaitanya worship in terms of theology and philosophy. As such, Chaitanya's position as the source of supreme love continued to be ambiguous and more a matter of personal faith and experience than the central feature in a system of belief. Even Narottamadasa, who was a passionate devotee of Chaitanya, tended to accept the Gosvami's view on Chaitanya (*upaya* rather than *upeya*) in his theological and doctrinal writings. In his *Nama-chintamani*, Narottama firmly declares that Krishna is the only object of worship, the Absolute Reality, and there is nothing which is comparable to him.[107] In the *Ragamala*, Narottama actually refers to Chaitanya as a *manjari*.[108]

Jiva died in 1592. After his death, the intellectual and spiritual leadership of Brindaban rapidly declined. During the seventeenth century there developed in Bengal several centres of Vaishnava learning and literature, such as Bishnupur, Srikhanda, Jajigram, Baghnapara, Santipur, Budhui, Baharampur and Gopiballabhpur, which emerged as sources of authoritative interpretation of Gauriya Vaishnavism. Apparently, in the final phase of the development of the Bhakti movement, the focus had shifted back to Bengal. But scholarly and literary pursuits in these centres were mostly confined to interpretation and translation into Bengali of the Gosvami texts. Even critics of the Gosvamis like Visvanatha Chakravarti did not try to develop an alternative to the Gosvami system. The doctrine of *Gaura-paramyavada* continued. *Padas* extolling the divinity of Chaitanya were composed in the eighteenth century or even later. But even before the middle of the seventeenth century, *Gaura-paramyavada* ceased to be a major source of inspiration. Gauriya Vaishnavism in Bengal came to be characterized by Krishna worship and confined to the framework of the Gosvami system. In this context Chaitanya came to be regarded as an *avatara* (incarnation) of Krishna who was born in Nabadwip with the specific purpose of propagating *bhakti*. As such, Chaitanya is an object of adoration in the path of devotion to Krishna who is the only Supreme Being. From the early decades of the seventeenth century till the end of the nineteenth century, a large number of Vaishnava temples were built in Bengal. Built in the regional Bengali style, these temples represent the continuity of a symbol of regional Bengali cultural identity in a stagnant architectural form.[109] The major bulk of these temples are dedicated to the worship of Krishna or Vishnu. Only a few of these temples were built for the worship of Chaitanya.

Notes and References

1. For discussion on the emergence of regional Bengali culture, see Niharranjan Ray, *Bangalir Itihas: Adi parva* (in Bengali) (Calcutta, 1949), pp. 723–56, 792–8, 829–66.

2. Dineschandra Sen, *Bangabhasa O Sahitya* (in Bengali), 4th edition (Calcutta, 1920), pp. 121–2, 158–60; Sukumar Sen, *Bangla Sahityer Itihas* (in Bengali), Vol. I, Part 1, 3rd edn (Calcutta 1959), pp. 137–8, 175–6.

3. Hitesranjan Sanyal, "Temple-Building in Bengal from the Fifteenth to the Nineteenth Century: A Study in Social Response to Technological Innovation", in Barun De (ed.), *Perspectives in Social Sciences* (Oxford University Press, Calcutta, 1977), pp. 120–68.

4. These salient features of the ideology and methodology of the Bhakti movement are indicated by the biographies of Chaitanya and a number of *padas* (lyrics) on Chaitanya composed by contemporary poets. Specific passages in the biographies and the relevant *padas* have been referred to below (see notes 55, 56, 57). For longer narratives relating to this subject, see *Chaitanya-bhagavat* (in Bengali) by Brindabanadasa (henceforth CB), Upendranath Mukhopadhyay (ed.), reprint of the 4th Basumati Sahitya Mandir edn (Calcutta, n.d.), II. 1, 2, 4, 5, 10, 12, 14, 17, 18, 19; III. 5; *Chaitanya-mangala* (in Bengali) by Lochanadasa, Bhagabandas Kavya–Vyakaranatirtha (ed.) (Nabadwip, Bengali Era (henceforth BE) 1388 = A.D. 1981), II. pp. 1, 2, 3, 5, 6, 8, 9, 10; *Chaitanya-mangala* (in Bengali) by Jayananda, Bimanbehari Majumdar and Sukhamay Mukhopadhyay (ed.), Asiatic Society edn (Calcutta, 1971), III. 4, 22.

5. *CB*, I. 8, pp. 57–8, II. 23, p. 225; *Chaitanya-mangala* by Jayananda, II. 30, pp. 4–16.

6. *CB*, II. 6, p. 131, II. 10, p. 156, III. 3, p. 286. III. 5, p. 303.

7. *CB*, III. 5, 6, 7; *Chaitanya-mangala* by Jayananda, IX, pp. 158–63.

8. For a detailed introduction to the esoteric sects, see Shashibhusan Dasgupta, *Obscure Religious Cults*, 3rd edn, reprint (Calcutta, 1976), pp. 3–34, 51–109; 191–205; Ray, *Bangalir Itihas*, pp. 635–98.

9. Narahari's Sahajiya inclination is clear from the *padas* composed by him. In his *padas* Narahari frequently uses the Sahajiya concepts of *rasa*, *rasika*, *svarupa*, *sahaja-svarupa*, *aropa*, and the Buddhist Sahajiya concepts of *sukha* and *vajra*. These *padas* are included in the *Krishnapadamrita-sindhu*, pp. 134–35 and Manindramohan Basu (compiled and annotated), *Sahajiya Sahitya* (in Bengali) (Calcutta, 1932), pp. 61–2, 65, 74, 90. Two specimens of Narahari's Sahajiya *padas* are given below: (1) *Sukhera sagare/Syamera piriti/Jojite paraha jabe/Jagatera sukh/Ekatra karile/Eta sukh pabe tabe/Dharama Karama/ Barai bishame/Anek jatane haya/Sahaja piriti/ Karaha jubati/Paibe Gokula Raya (Krishna-padamrta-sindhu*, p. 135. (2) *Sahajera katha suna lo sai/kahiba tare* (Basu, *Sahajiya Sahitya* [in Bengali], p. 74). These *padas* envisage the doctrine of *Gaura-nagara* and the complementary doctrine of *Nadiya-nagari*

propounded by Narahari. Narahari's disciple Lochanadasa was held by the Sahajiyas as an authoritative poet of their sect. A *pada* composed by Lochana has been quoted in the famous Sahajiya text *Vivarta-vilasa* (in Bengali) for illustrating the significance of Sahajiya worship with reference to *rupa* and *rasa*. (*Vivarta-vilasa* by Akinchanadasa, Bidyaratna Jantra edn [Calcutta, B.E. 1311 = A.D. 1904–5], III. p. 48.)

10. Bansibadana propagated the *Sahajiya Rasaraja sadhana* which he inherited from his father Chhakari Chatta (see Sukumar Sen, *Bangla Sahityer Itihas* [in Bengali] Vol. I, part 2, 3rd edn [Calcutta, 1975], p. 65, 400–1). For details of the *Rasaraja* doctrine, see note 26.

11. *Vivarta-vilasa*, I. p. 2. See also Bimanbehari Majumdar, *Chaitanyachariter Upadan* (in Bengali), 2nd edn (Calcutta, 1959), p. 536. For Svarupa's Sahajiya connections, see S. Sen, *Bangla Sahityer Itihas*, p. 43.

12. *Chaitanya-chandrodaya-natakam* (in Sanskrit) by Kavi Karnapura, Jibananda Vidyasagara (ed.), Saraswati Jantra edn (Calcutta, 1885), VII. 2.

13. *Sri Sri Krishna-chaitanya-charitamritam* (in Sanskrit) by Murari Gupta (usually known as Murari Gupta's *Karcha*, henceforth *Karcha*), 3rd Nalini Press edn (Calcutta, 445 Gauravda = A.D. 1931–32), II. 2. 8–10, II. 4.4, II. 5. 14, II. 9. 18–23, II. 12. 12–17; *CB*, II. 6. p. 129–30, II. 9. p. 146–7;

Chaitanya-charitamrita (in Sanskrit) by Kavi Karnapura (usually referred to as *Mahakavya*, henceforth *Mahakavya*), Radharaman Jantra edn (Baharampur), VI. 26, VII. 32–5; *pada* by Govinda Ghosh in *Gaura–pada–tarangini*, Jagadbandhu Bhadra (compiled), Mrinalkanti Ghosh (ed.), 2nd Bangiya Sahitya Parisat edn (Calcutta, B.E. 1341 = A.D. 1934–35), p. 150.

14. *Karcha* II. 10. 16–20; *CB*, III. 10, p. 331–7.

15. *Karcha*, I. 12. 19.

16. *Chaitanya-chandamrita* (in Sanskrit) by Prabodhananda Sarasvati, Anandimohan Gosvami (ed.), Gauriya Vaishnava Sammilani edn (Calcutta, B.E. 1360 = A.D. 1953–54), *sloka* 58.

17. *Chaitanya-chandrodaya*, I. 7. 28; *Mahakavya*, I, 8. 17.

18. In the opening section of *mangalacharana* and *lilasutra-varnana* of the *Chaitanya-bhagavat*, Brindabanadasa explicitly calls Chaitanya Mahesvara (Supreme Being), Narayana (Vishnu) and Bhagavan (God). This sets the tone of the entire text which explicates Chaitanya's identity with the Absolute Reality. Similarly in the opening verse of *Chaitanya-mangala* (in Bengali), Lochanadasa describes Chaitanya as being *purnabatirnah* (full incarnation of the God) and describes the life of the Master in this light.

19. Sushil Kumar De, *The Early History of the Vaisnava Faith and Movement in Bengal*, 2nd edn (Calcutta, 1961), pp. 124, 230–31.

20. *Gaura–ganoddesa–dipika* (in Sanskrit) by Kavi Karnapura, 5th Radharaman Jantra edn (Baharampur, Murshidabad, B.E. 1305 = A.D. 1912–13), sloka 10–11.

21. See, for example, *Sri Sri Pada–kalpataru* (henceforth *PK*) Satish Chandra Ray (ed.), (Calcutta, B.E. 1304 = 1897–98), *padas* by Narahari Sarkar (*pada* nos 307, 316, 408, 421, 1746, 1902, 2259), Sibananda Sena (nos 2127, 2355), Paramananda Sena (no. 2120). Also *padas* by Basu Ghosh in *Basu Ghosher Padavali* (in Bengali), Malabika Chaki (ed.), Bangiya Sahitya Parisat edn (Calcutta, B.E. 1368 = 1961), *pada* nos 16, 17, 18, 23, 24, 27, 28, 35, 38, 44, 56, 63.

22. The doctrine was propagated in the Bengali and Sanskrit works of the associates and followers of Chaitanya but it was formulated in the Sanskrit works of Murari Gupta, Prabodhananda Sarasvati and Paramananda Sena, who is more well known as Kavi Karnapura. These works have been referred to earlier. See also Majumdar, *Chaitanyachariter Upadan*, pp. 112, 175–79; De, *The Early History of the Vaisnava Faith and Movement in Bengal*, p. 229.

23. *Karcha*. IV. 14. 12–4; *Narottama–vilasa* (in Bengali) by Narahari Chakravarti, Kamalasan Jantra edn (Calcutta, B.E. 1262 = A.D. 1855–56), III. pp. 45, 51, V. pp. 76, 80. Sixteenth-century and seventeenth-century Chaitanya

images are still found in Kulia, Guptipara, Kalna, Nabadwip, Katwa and Srikhanda.

24. Majumdar, *Chaitanyachariter Upadan*, pp. 112, 435.

25. Sukumar Sen, *Bangla Sahityer Itihas*, p. 401.

26. See note 10. *Bansi-siksha* was composed in 1716–17. Divided into four *ullasas* (chapters), the text gives a detailed discourse on the *Rasaraja* doctrine and Bansibadana's position as 'the enjoyed' through *ullasa* I, II, III and half of the fourth. See Premadasa, *Bansi-siksha*. Nemaichand Goswami (ed.), Swastik Mudranalay edn (Calcutta, n.d.).

27. For *Gaura–nagara* and *Nadiya–nagari* doctrines, see De, *The Early History of the Vaisnava Faith and Movement in Bengal*, pp. 65–6; introduction to *Chaitanya-mangala* by Lochanadasa, p. IV–V.

28. *Chaitanya-chandramrita, sloka* 132.

29. See, for example, in *PK, padas* by Narahari Sarkar (no. 103), Gobinda Ghosh (no. 1597); *padas* in *Basu Ghoser Padavali*, no. 34, 70, 74, 75, 76, 78–106; *pada* by Jadunandan Chakravarti in *Bhakti–ratnakara* (in Bengali, henceforth *BR*) by Narahari Chakravarti, Nandalal Vidyasagar (ed.), Gaudiya Mission edn (Calcutta, 1960), XII. 2819–2823, 2851–2857. Lochanadasa composed *Chaitanya-mangala* with the specific intention of vindicating the *nagarabhava* doctrine.

30. *CB*, III. 5. pp. 303–14, III. 6.314–17; *Chaitanya-mangala* by Jayananda, III. 7.

31. *Chaitanya-charitamrita* (in Bengali) by Krishnadasa Kaviraja, Nityananda Goswami (ed.), 3rd Sulabh Library edn (Calcutta, Caitanyavda 441 = A.D. 1927), II. 23. p. 261.

32. For biographical details of the six Brindaban Gosvamis, see Nareschandra Jana, *Brindabaner Chhay Gosvami* (in Bengali) (Calcutta, 1970).

33. For a comprehensive introduction to the works of the Gosvamis, see De, *Early History of the Vaisnava Faith*, chapters IV, V, VI.

34. *CB*, II. 13. p. 169, II. 24. p. 230.

35. *CB*, II. 3. p. 119, III. 7. pp. 317–18, III. 8. pp. 323, 325.

36. *CB*, II. 24. pp. 228, 230–3.

37. Brindabanadasa, who was an ardent follower of Nityananda, has condemned *Gaura-nagaravada* (*CB*. I. 10. p. 78). Narahari was one of the closest associates of Chaitanya. But Brindabanadasa does not refer to Narahari and Murari, and Karnapura practically ignores his role. Possibly this is due to their aversion to the *Gaura-nagara* doctrine.

38. The split in the Bhakti movement and the consequent flux is indicated by the *Chaitanya-chandramrita* (*sloka* 38). For details, see Niradbehari Nath, *Narottamadasa O Tanhar Rachanavali* (in Bengali) (Calcutta, 1975), *Alocana*, pp. 123–31.

39. There were fifty-eight poets among the associates of Chaitanya, all of whom have composed Bengali *padas* or Sanskrit *stotras* on the Master. More prominent among these poets are Narahari Sarkar, Basu Ghosh, Ramananda Basu, Sivananda Sena and Prabodhananda Sarasvati. Several biographical works, both in Sanskrit and Bengali, were produced by the associates of Chaitanya or their disciples. They include the following:

    Sanskrit:

    (a) *Sri Krishna-chaitanya-caritamritam* by Murari Gupta,

    (b) *Chaitanya-charitamrita (Mahakavya)* by Kavi Karnapura,

    (c) *Chaitanya-chandrodaya-natakam* by Kavi Karnapura.

    Bengali:

    (a) *Chaitanya-bhagavat* by Brindabanadasa,

    (b) *Gauranga-vijaya* by Churamanidasa,

    (c) *Chaitanya-mangala* by Lochanadasa,

    (d) *Chaitanya-mangala* by Jayananda.

40. Paramananda Sena (Kavi Karnapura) was junior contemporary of Chaitanya and the son of Sivananda Sena. Karnapura was a man of considerable literary and scholarly talents and a versatile author. He has written extensively on the life and teachings of Chaitanya and on the faith of the Bhakti movement. These include the *Mahakavya* and the *Nataka* referred to earlier, *Alamkara-kaustubha*

(on devotional sentiments), *Gaura-ganoddesa-dipika* (hagiology), *Ananda-Vrindavana-champa* (interpretation of *Krishnalila*) and a commentary on the *Srimad-bhagavat*. Karnapura sought to systematize the faith within a theoretical framework. The only other attempt towards theoretical discourse is the *bhajanamrita*, a theological text by Narahari Sarkar. Karnapura's works do not appear to have received sufficient organisational support from the adherents of the Bhakti movement and were completely overshadowed by the works of the Brindaban Gosvamis which provided the canons of Bengal Vaishnavism.

41. For the ancestry of Sanatana and Rupa, see the family history given by Jiva Gosvami at the end of his *Laghu-Vaishnava-toshini*. According to the *Bhakti-ratnakara*, Sanatana and Rupa had set up a colony of Bhatta (Karnataka) Brahmans near Ramkeli in the vicinity of the city of Gaur where they lived while serving under the Sultan. Their social and religious interactions were confined to these Brahman families (*BR*, I. 592–95).

42. See in *PK*, *padas* by Murari Gupta (no. 749), Narahari Sarkar (nos 103, 307, 316, 408, 421, 853, 1746, 1902) *padas* by Basu Ghosh in *Basu Ghosher Padavali* (nos 42, 45, 46, 57); *Chaitanya-mangala* by Lochanadasa, II. 13. 637–9, Appendix, *pada* nos 8, 9.

43. *Karcha*. II. 4.4, 5.14, III. 2.9, 19–23 *CB*, II. 3, p. 115, II. 6, pp. 129–30, II. 9, pp. 146–47, II. 19, pp. 198, II. 20, p. 204; *pada* by Basu Ghosh in *PK*, nos 936, 1368; *pada* by Govinda Ghosh in *Gaurapada-tarangini*. p. 160; *padas* by Basu Ghosh in *Basu Ghoser Padavali*, nos 16–18, 23, 24, 27, 28, 35, 38, 44, 56, 63.

44. See notes 42 and 15, 16, 17, 18, 21.

45. *CB*, II. 6, p. 131, II. 10, p. 156, III. 4, p. 286, III. 5, p. 303.

46. Jana, *Brindabaner Chhay Gosvami*, p. 150.

47. *Karcha*, III. 15, 14–16.

48. *Karcha*, IV. 15–17.

49. CC, III. 6, pp. 325–35.

50. See in *PK*, *padas* by Narahari Sarkar (nos 799, 820, 832, 840, 1643); *padas* by Basu Ghosh in *Basu Ghoser Padavali*, nos 127, 143. For elaborate description of Chaitanya's *Radha-bhava* in Puri, see CC, III. 14, 15, 18, 19.

51. *Chaitanya-chandramrita. sloka* 13, 109; *pada* by Narahari Sarkar in *PK*. no. 2259 *padas* by Basu Ghosh in *Basu Ghoser Padavali*. nos 1, 13; CC. I. 8, p. 137. Raghunathadasa Gosvami also believed in this theory (see De, *The Early History of the Vaisnava Faith and Movement in Bengal*, p. 425).

52. As indicated earlier, Chaitanya demonstrated *Radha-bhava* before he became a *sannyasi*. But according to Krishnadasa Kaviraja, *Radha-bhava* in the Master sharply accentuated after

his long discourse with Ray Ramananda who convinced Chaitanya of his identity with Radha (CC, I.8).

53. For a short introduction to the Vaishnava sects, see D.C. Sircar, "Vaishnavism" in R.C. Majumdar (ed.), *The History and Culture of the Indian People: The Struggle for Empire*, 2nd edn (Bombay, 1966), pp. 435–42; R.C. Majumdar, "Religion" in R.C. Majumdar (ed.), *The History and Culture of the Indian People: The Delhi Sultanate*, 2nd edn (Bombay, 1967), pp. 557–72.

54. De, *The Early History of the Vaisnava Faith and Movement in Bengal*, pp. 421–47.

55. *CB*, II. 1, p. 95, II. 12. p. 165, II. 18. pp. 189, 191–94, III. V. pp. 304–5, 307; *Chaitanya-mangala* by Lochanadasa, II. 434–41, 448–63; *padas* by Jadunandana Chakravarti, *BR*, XII, 3054–62, 3077–82; *pada* by Ramananda Basu. *BR*, XII, 3426–29.

56. *Chaitanya-chandrodaya*, I, 30.

57. *Chaitanya-mangala* by Jayananda, III. 22. 2–6.

58. De, *The Early History of the Vaisnava Faith and Movement in Bengal*, pp. 174–77, 369–77.

59. De, *The Early History of the Vaisnava Faith and Movement in Bengal*, p. 178.

60. *CB*. I. 1. pp. 1–5, I. 12, p. 92. II. 13, p. 227; *pada* by Basu Ghosh in *Basu Ghoser Padavali*, no. 54; *Chaitanya-mangala* by Lochanadasa, II. 4, 205–12.

61. See in *PK*, *pada* by Narahari Sarkar (no. 2122), *pada* by Paramananda Gupta (no. 2120);

pada by Jadunandana Chakravarti in *BR*. XII. 2803–07, 3054–62.

62. *See* note 29.

63. *CB*. II. 5, p. 125, II. 10, p. 16, II. 17, p. 188, III. 5, p. 303, III. 6, p. 316; *padas* by Basu Ghosh, *Basu Ghoser Padavali*, no. 45, 63.

64. *Gaura-ganoddesa-dipika*, *sloka* 30 ff.

65. This is the general socio-religious attitude of the text. For specific references, see summary of the text in De, *The Early History of the Vaisnava Faith and Movement in Bengal*, pp. 411–520.

66. *Haribhakti-vilasa* by Gopala Bhatta, Puridas Mahasay (ed.), Sachinath Ray Chaturdharin edn., (Aloya, Mymensingh, 1946), XI, 746, 762–65.

67. *Haribhakti-vilasa*. I. 47–52.

68. *CC*, II. 19. p. 221–26, II. 20. pp. 229–262.

69. *CC*, I. 1, p. 2.

70. De, *The Early History of the Vaisnava Faith and Movement in Bengal*, 93–4, 100, 427; B. Majumdar, *Chaitanyachariter Upadan*, pp. 382–84.

71. Chaitanya occasionally demonstrated *Radha-bhava* in Nabadwip (see note 42). This indicates his inclination to the *raganuga* way in terms of *madhura rasa* from the early stage of his religious career.

72. Jana, *Brindabaner Chhay Gosvami*, pp. 64–5, 68–9.

73. *Prema-vilasa* (in Bengali) by Nityanandadasa, 2nd Radharaman Jantra edn. (Baharampur, Murshidabad, B.E. 1318 = A.D. 1911–12), XII,

pp. 143–60; *NV*, III. pp. 40–1. For date, see Nath, *Narottamadasa O Tanhar Rachanavali*, p. 16; Sukhamay Mukhopadhyay, *Chaitanyadeva* (in Bengali) (Calcutta, 1984), p. 90.

74. *Prema-vilasa*, XII, p. 134–43; *NV*, II, pp. 38–9.

75. *NV*, III, p. 41; *Sri Sri Syamananda Prakasa* (in Bengali), by Krishnacharanadasa Gopala-Govindananda Deva-Gosvami (ed.), Syamanandi Gadi edn. (Gopiballabhpur, Medinipur, B.E. 1384 = A.D. 1957–8), IV. 145–49, V, VI; VII, VIII, XI, XII, XV, XVI.

76. *BR*, VII. 204–26, 259–93, VIII. 506–637, IX. 260–387, 495–575, X, 89–187, 292–329; *NV*, IX. p. 188.

77. *NV*, III. pp. 49–55, IV. pp. 59–73, V. pp. 74–83.

78. Nath, *Narottamadasa O Tanhar Rachanavali*, pp. 15–16.

79. *NV*. VI. p. 97, 100, 104, 105, 106, 109, 135, 136, 178.

80. *NV*. VII. p. 115.

81. *NV*. VII. pp. 114–15.

82. For example, see *pada* nos 67 to 77 in *Basu Ghosher Padavali*.

83. Swami Prajnanananda, *Padavali Kirtaner Itihas*. Vol. I (Calcutta, 1970), pp. 34–5, 119.

84. This has been clearly explicated by Jayananda in his *Chaitanya-mangala*, III. 22. 2–6. See also *CC* I. 1, p. 5, I. 3, p. 13, I. 7, pp. 38–41.

85. B. Majumdar, *Chaitanyachariter Upadan*, 564.

86. *NV*. VII, pp. 118–21; *Prema-vilasa* specifically says that in the Kheturi festival songs on Chaitanya were followed by songs on Krishna (XIX. p. 318).

87. *Nama-chintamani* by Narottamadasa in Nath, pp. 527–28, 531.

88. *NV*, VIII. pp. 1–37.

89. *NV*, VI. p. 90, IX. pp. 189–90, X. 193–4, 197–204, 213–4.

90. For Syamananda's caste, see *BR*, I. 351–4. Syamananda's principal disciple Rasikananda was Brahman.

91. Nath, *Narottamadasa O Tanhar*, p. 144.

92. CC, II. 8. p. 131.

93. Nath, *Narottamadasa O Tanhar*, 94–5; *Prema-vilasa*, VI. pp. 65–6.

94. Nath, *Narottamadasa O Tanhar*, pp. 95–117.

95. *Gaura-ganoddesa-dipika*, *sloka* 180–207; Nath, *Narottamadasa O Tanhar*, p. 95.

96. Nath, *Narottamadasa O Tanhar*, pp. 102–17; *Ragamala* by Narottamadasa, pp. 633–43.

97. Dasgupta, *Obscure Religious Cults*, pp. 113–34.

98. Dasgupta, *Obscure Religious Cults*, p. 121.

99. Dasgupta, *Obscure Religious Cults*, p. 120–22.

100. Dasgupta, *Obscure Religious Cults*, p. 140.

101. Sukumar Sen, "Srikhander Sampraday O Chandidas" (in Bengali), in *Bichitra Sahitya* (Calcutta, 1956), p. 129.

102. Nath, *Narottamadasa O Tanhar*, pp. 110–11; *Ragamala* by Narottamadasa, p. 639.

103. See, for example, the *pada* by Ray-sekhara in the *Siddanta-chandrodaya* (pp. 157–58) as quoted in Sukumar Sen, "Srikhander Sampraday O Chandidas", p. 122.

104. *Jemati nritya (nitya)/Sahaja sunian/Samanya dehete Jage/Na jane maram/Kare acharan/ Kebal rourabe maje/.... Brajabhava jaian/ Gopianugata sar/Nijadehe jeba/Ghatay sahaj/ Acharite kare as/Bhane Vidyapati/Koti janma tar/Rourabete habe bas.* Quoted in Sukumar Sen, "Srikhander Sampraday O Chandidas" in *Vaishnaviya Nibandha* (Calcutta, 1970), p. 217–18.

105. Sukumar Sen, "Srikhander Sampraday O Chandidas", p. 218.

106. Sudhir Chakravarti, "Maner Manuser Gabhir Nirjan Pathe" (in Bengali), *Ekshan*, Saradiya, B.E. 1391 = A.D. 1984, p. 19; Sudhir Chakravarti, *Sahebdhani Sampradaya O Tader Gan* (in Bengali) (Calcutta, 1985), p. 95.

107. *Nama-chintamani*, in Nath, *Narottamadasa O Tanhar Rachanavali*, p. 527.

108. *Ragamala* by Narottamadasa, p. 639.

109. Sanyal, "Temple-Building in Bengal from the Fifteenth to the Nineteenth Century" p. 148–55.

Index